Soups, Stews
& Quickbreads

Soups, Stews & Quickbreads

*495 Quick & Easy Recipes
from Around the World*

Jan Thomson

CLEAR LIGHT PUBLISHERS
SANTA FE, NEW MEXICO

Clear Light Publishers
823 Don Diego, Santa Fe, NM 87501

First Edition
10 9 8 7 6 5 4 3 2 1

Library of Congress Cataloging-in-Publication Data

Thomson, Jan, 1952-
    Soups, stews & quickbreads : 450 quick and easy recipes from around the world / Jan Thomson.
        p. cm.
    Includes index.
    ISBN 1-57416-002-8 (pbk.)
    1. Soups. 2. Stews. 3. Bread. 4. Quick and easy cookery. 5. Cookery, International. I. Title.
TX757.T48   1998
641.8'13—dc21   98-11904
                                                              CIP

Cover photograph by David Thomson

DEDICATION

To my wonderful husband, the taste king.
Thank you for being patient with the
long hours dedicated to this book,
your unending love, and being
the best friend I've ever had and
much more!

ACKNOWLEDGMENTS

There are many people to thank, but the first who comes to mind is this book's publisher, Harmon Houghton. I'd also like to thank Clear Light editor Sara Held. Thank you. I will never forget that first phone call.

And thanks to—

My sister Liz, one of my best friends, for unending fun and silliness as we tried to figure out why the computer did some of the rude things it did.

My husband David for your constant love and encouragement.

Edith, my friend and mother-in-law, a lady who knows more about cooking than most.

My Mom, who launched my career in cooking when I was four by teaching me to have fun in the kitchen.

All the guys who taught me how to simplify a recipe. By teaching you, you taught me.

My brother Larry for the help that summer, and for your comedic relief. Yes, they are still making PB&J sandwiches on Buckhorn Drive.

Last but not least, I want to thank my kitties for being so persistent about making me take breaks from the sometimes constant writing. Thanks for standing in front of my computer screen and lying down on my keyboard.

Contents

INTRODUCTION

So often when I reach for a cookbook, I am often overwhelmed by the complicated recipes. When I'm in a hurry I don't want to read a chapter when a few simple words would have gotten the message across. In my quest for simple recipes, I have taken somewhat complicated recipes and simplified them, so that you have the directions almost at a glance. I found when looking at a recipe you have different groups of food that need to be mixed together, cooked together, or added at different times, so I thought it simplest to put the ingredients into groups and number them. Within each recipe, you will find #1 ingredients, first group; #2 ingredients, second group; and so on. These are simple recipes because each group of ingredients have fast, simple directions so you know what to do with each group of food right away.

I have suggested Toppers (a garnish) for each soup and a suggested quick bread to serve alongside. A good thing about soups is that you ingest the liquid the food is cooked in. Therefore, you get all those good nutrients. Because you want to maintain the quality of your food, cooking times may vary for people who prefer a crisper vegetable. You can reduce the cooking time or add the vegetable of choice toward the end of the cooking time. For vegetarians, you have the option of using veggie stock instead of chicken, beef, or fish, with equally delicious results.

In Chapter 1, I have included a lot of helpful tips on substitutions, cooking terms, weights and measurements, how to choose a good soup pot, a list of toppers (garnishes) for the soups, and some fail-safe soup stocks, plus a lot of information and suggestions that I have found handy for working in the kitchen.

This book started 10 years ago with the urgings of family and friends. I started organizing the collected recipes that I have used over the years.

I enjoy cooking, and there have been many recipes that have stumped me. Instead of getting mad because I might have ruined a meal, I started teaching myself shortcuts and easier ways to work with some difficult recipes. This book is the result. There is no better feeling for me than to hand someone who is hungry a hot bowl of food and a slice of good homemade bread.

Chapter 1

ALL KINDS OF TIPS

Those Magic Bricks and My Friend Marthabell

When I was 11 years old, we fell upon some hard times and my mother had to go to work full time. She employed a woman to take care of me, my two sisters, and my little brother. The woman's name was Marthabell, and she was the largest person I'd ever seen, with a heart just as big. I was absolutely fascinated by Marthabell, being a skinny little white child. I think initially I was fascinated with her because she was black, and always smelled of Juicy Fruit gum, and she had a powerful singing voice that would put the sweetest song-bird to shame.

Marthabell loved to cook and would sing old southern gospel songs as she cooked. Another thing I remember, was her ability to have fun in the kitchen. She would start off each recipe with her brick dance. With two red bricks, one in each hand, she would dance around the kitchen singing about those bricks. Those were her cooking bricks, and she wouldn't or couldn't cook without them. "Cooks it even, dahlin'," she'd say. "Girl, nothin' won't burn." She'd lay those two bricks on the gas burner and turn the flame on high with the bricks slightly apart. I remember staring at those blue flames licking around the bricks. She would then prepare the food to cook. In the pot it would go and she would say, "Don't have to worry 'bout it 'til time to eat!"

Needless to say I have used red bricks to cook on and I have never had anything burn. I will, on occasion, send my cats running, trying to get a grip on the linoleum of the kitchen floor, 'cause I cut loose and do the brick dance myself. Thanks, Marthabell!

I place the dry, red bricks on the burner slightly apart and turn the flame on low for 5 minutes, medium for 5 minutes, high 10 minutes, then back to low. Then keeping the flame on low, I set the pot of food on top of the bricks. It does a beautiful job of simmering. I can then go on about my business. The bricks will glow on the bottom. This works on electric stoves as well.

Just remember the bricks have to be completely dry or they will break.

Soup Pots

A good soup pot is not hard to find. Knowing what to spend your money on is a different story. In my ignorance I looked for a good bargain that was advertised as a non-stick stewing pot for $9.99. Those "non-stick" stewing pots can burn boiling water. Punch some holes in it and they make beautiful planters! What follows is what I've learned.

Aluminum, if heavy enough, can be a good heat conductor. Foods, however, may react chemically and the inside of your pot may turn black, especially when cooking tomatoes.

Porcelain or enamels can chip, be hard to clean, and may discolor over a period of time.

Copper is beautiful, and conducts heat well, but can be expensive. It must be lined with tin or stainless steel. Otherwise it can be toxic and will react chemically with most foods. I do have a set that hangs on the wall (a garage sale bargain) and are used for special sauces.

Stainless steel is by far my favorite. It can also be expensive, but it will last forever. A heavy stainless steel pot is hard to beat. They do not react with foods, are easy to clean, and conduct heat evenly. I have one 16-quart pot that has been in the family for almost 30 years.

Tips on Soup Making

- Always read the entire recipe first.
- Make sure you have all the ingredients before you start. It is always easier if you put the ingredients in groups on your counter.
- Make sure you have a big enough soup pot. Eight- to twelve-quart pots should do fine for most soup recipes.
- Do all your slicing and dicing before you begin to cook.
- Taste, taste, taste! as you go, so that you may add ingredients if necessary.
- Soups can be many different consistencies. If you don't like yours, add more stock or water to thin the soup. Or, mix cornstarch and water and add this to your soup to make it thicker. Usually three tablespoons of cornstarch to a half cup water will do it. If you end up not using it, it can be stored, covered in the fridge, for a couple of weeks.

Thickeners for Soup

Corn starch and water
Heavy cream or half-and-half
Lentils
Macaroni

Potatoes
Rice
Sour cream
Split peas

List of Toppers (soup garnishes)

Avocado, diced
Black olives
Butter
Cheese croutons
Chinese noodles, fried
Chives
Crackers
Crisp bacon
Cucumbers, sliced
Dijon mustard
Dill weed
Dumplings
French fried onions
Fritos
Garlic croutons
Grated carrots
Grated cheeses
   Cheddar
   Swiss
   Mozzarella

   Edam
   Colby
   Parmesan
   Sour cream
Green bell pepper, diced
Green olives
Hard-boiled eggs, sliced
Horseradish
Melba rounds
Onion, diced
Oyster crackers
Parsley
Popcorn
Red bell pepper, diced
Salsa
Sesame seeds
Tomatoes, diced
Tortilla chips
Tiny shrimp
Yellow bell pepper, diced

Toppers for Cold Soups

Apple sauce
Apples, diced
Blueberries
Granola
Grapes
Ice cream
Jellies
Kiwi slices
Lemon slices
Lime slices
Mandarin orange slices

Mint leaves
Nutmeg
Orange slices
Peanuts
Pineapple slices
Raspberries
Strawberries
Toasted almond slivers
Toasted coconut
Whipped cream

Some Substitutions

IF YOU DON'T WANT TO USE	YOU CAN USE
Bacon or ham	Turkey bacon, or smoked turkey ham
Butter	You can use a small amount of butter for flavor; or use olive or canola for "heart smart" recipes when you sauté.
Cheeses	You can generally find lowfat cheeses that will melt evenly. Be aware that some nonfat cheeses cannot be cooked. Check the package directions.
Dried beans	1 15-ounce can, usually drained, should be enough to substitute for about 1/2 cup dried beans. Reduce the stock in the recipe by half.
Eggs	1 egg equals about 3 tablespoons egg substitute.
Fresh garlic	Bottled, minced garlic
Fresh vegetables	Frozen is the next choice because most frozen vegetables are blanched and flash–frozen. Canned would be a second choice. Unless indicated by the recipe, you can add the veggie while still frozen. Just add a few minutes cooking time.
Half-and-half	1% or 2% milk (you can also use skim milk)
Hamburger	Ground chicken or turkey
Heavy cream	Half-and-half
Herbs and spices	Fresh is always best but some are hard to find, especially in my Montana grocery stores. Recipe will indicate if you can substitute dried or not. For most herbs use flakes if you can; ground will be indicated otherwise. If the recipe looks good but you don't like garlic, use a little extra onion or just use your imagination.
Ice cream	Lowfat or nonfat

IF YOU DON'T WANT TO USE	YOU CAN USE
Milk products	15–ounce can of undrained navy beans, pureed will yield about 2 cups. Mix according to the directions for the milk products in the recipe. Gives a wonderful creamy texture and appearance.
Minute rice	Your favorite long-cooking rice. Use the same amount. Just precook and add at the end of the soups cooking time, and let heat back through.
Oil or butter	Same amount of applesauce.
Pork sausage	Chicken or turkey sausage
Soup stocks, homemade	Soup bases can be found in the soup section of the grocery store. Do be careful—they usually have a lot of added salt. Look for low-salt stocks.
Sour cream	Lowfat sour cream. Always check the directions on nonfat sour cream. Some products are not recommended for cooking. (See label.)
Whipping cream	Cool Whip Lite or nonfat

How the Soup Recipes Work

#1 Ingredients
The first group of ingredients to be used or cooked first.

#2 Ingredients
The second group to be mixed together, or added.

#3 Ingredients
The third group is usually an ingredient that cooks fast, and will flavor or thicken the soup.

#4 Ingredients
These usually have special directions.

All serving sizes are measured for 16-ounce servings, about 2 cups. These are approximated according to absorption and shrinkage that occurs in all cooking.

How the Bread Recipes Work

#1 Ingredients
These are usually the dry ingredients, to be mixed together with a wire whisk.

#2 Ingredients
This group is usually the soft butter or margarine, to be blended into the flour with a pastry blender. Or, the wet ingredients to be mixed together with a wire whisk.

#3 Ingredients
The third group is sometimes seeds to be put on top of the bread or an ingredient to be brushed on.

#4 Ingredients
The fourth group will usually have special directions.

When your bread comes out of the oven, turn it out to a wire rack and lay it on its side. Let it cool before you slice it. Get a good bread knife if you don't have one. It makes slicing a lot easier and will not tear the bread.

Cooking Terms

Blend: To mix two or more ingredients until thoroughly incorporated.
Brown: To turn food surface brown through applied heat from frying, broiling, or baking.
Brush: To spread a coating of a sauce, fat, or glaze on the surface of a food with a brush, soft cloth or a paper towel.
Chill: Place the food in a refrigerator until it is cold throughout.
Chop: To cut food into small uniform pieces.
Cool: To let heated food stand at room temperature until it reaches room temperature.
Dice: To cut into small cubes smaller than those chopped.
Drain: To separate a liquid from a food. Tools include a strainer or colander.
Flour: To dust the surface lightly with flour.
Garnish: To add another touch of food to a prepared food for decoration, contrast, flavor, and texture.
Knead: To manipulate dough with the hands by pressing with the palms and folding until the dough becomes smooth and elastic.
Mix: To combine two or more ingredients. Tools include a mixing spoon, wire whisk, rotary beater, and electric mixer.

Pack: To press in a cup removing all the air.

Peel: To pull off the rind or outer covering of an orange, banana, or potato.

Sauté: To brown or cook in a small amount of fat.

Shred: To tear or cut food into thin strips. Tools include knife and grater.

Seed: To remove seeds.

Weight and Measure Equivalents

2 teaspoons	1 dessert spoon
3 teaspoons	1 tablespoon
4 tablespoons	¼ cup
16 tablespoons	1 cup
1 cup	½ pint
4 cups	1 quart
2 quarts	½ gallon
1 egg	3 tablespoons
2 cups ground or chopped meat	1 pound
Measure for dairy	
½ cup butter soft	1 stick butter
6 tablespoons cream cheese	3-ounce package
1¼ cups grated cheese	¼ pound hard cheese
1¼ cups shredded soft cheese	4 ounces soft cheese
2 cups whipped cream	1 cup heavy cream
Measure for fruit	
1 cup sliced apple	1 large apple
1½ cups mashed banana	3 medium bananas
2-3 tablespoons fresh squeezed lemon juice	1 medium lemon
2 teaspoons grated lemon zest	1 medium lemon
1½ to 2 teaspoons grated lime zest	1 medium lime
1¾ cups berries	1 pint berries
3½ to 4 cups berries	1 quart berries
Measure for Pasta or Rice	
2 to 2½ cups cooked pasta	¼ pound uncooked pasta
about 3 cups cooked rice	1 cup uncooked rice

Soup Stocks

Remember to leave all the veggies whole. Soup stocks will be listed as an ingredient. (Soup bases can be substituted, but watch out for extra salt.)

Chicken Stock

6 quarts water
6 pounds chicken necks, backs, gizzards, wings
1 dried bay leaf
3 stalks celery with leaves
8 to 10 peppercorns

1 teaspoon thyme, dried or fresh
2 large onions, peeled
6 cloves garlic
3 carrots, peeled
3 leeks, washed (whites only)
1 small turnip, peeled

Simmer 2 hours, uncovered. Makes about 24 cups.

Beef Stock

6 quarts water
6 pounds beef soup bones with drippings, roasted in the oven 30 minutes at 400 degrees
1 bay leaf
3 medium onions, peeled

3 stalks celery with leaves
8 to 10 peppercorns
4 sprigs parsley
4 cloves garlic
2 medium tomatoes, cut in quarters

Simmer 2 hours, uncovered. Makes about 24 cups.

Fish Stock

6 quarts water
3 pounds strong smelling fish (such as perch)
3 carrots
3 onions, peeled
4 stalks celery with leaves

6 cloves garlic
1 bay leaf
1 teaspoon thyme, dried or fresh
8 to 10 peppercorns
4 cups white wine
3- x 3-inch lemon skin

Simmer 1 hour, partially uncovered. Makes about 24 cups.

"Finishing" Stock

- Always filter your stocks first by taking all the meat and veggies out with a slotted spoon.
- Fold a piece of cheese cloth in half, then in half again. Drape it over your spaghetti strainer. Pour the stock over the strainer with a pot underneath to catch the liquid.
- For veggie stock, omit the meat or chicken.
- After clarifying your stocks, chill completely and remove any fat that solidified on the top.

Chapter 2

SOUPS MADE WITH VEGGIES

Veggie Minestrone

about 7 16-ounce servings

#1 Ingredients
2 tablespoons olive oil
1/2 cup onion, chopped
1/4 cup celery, sliced
1/4 cup carrots, sliced
1/2 cup fresh zucchini, diced
1/4 cup frozen corn
2 cups fresh spinach, chopped, or
　1 10-ounce package frozen
　spinach, chopped
1 teaspoon fresh garlic, minced,
　or 1/2 teaspoon garlic powder

#2 Ingredients
6 cups chicken stock
1 14-ounce can stewed tomatoes
1 15-ounce can kidney beans,
　rinsed and drained
salt and pepper to taste

#3 Ingredient
1 cup uncooked large-shell pasta

Topper/grated Romano cheese

- Cook and drain the #3 ingredient and set aside.
- Sauté the #1 ingredients until just tender, add to the #2 ingredients, and bring to a simmer for 20 minutes. Add the #3 ingredient, let reheat, and serve.

Goes well with *Cheese and Beer Bread with a Kick*, page 144.

Everything-Green Soup

about 4 16-ounce servings

#1 Ingredients
6 cups chicken stock
1 cup fresh zucchini, diced
1/2 cup fresh green beans, sliced,
　or 1/2 cup frozen cut green
　beans
1/2 cup fresh shelled sweet peas or
　1/2 cup frozen peas
2 cups packed fresh spinach, or 1
　10-ounce package frozen
　spinach, chopped
1/2 cup green onions, sliced
salt and white pepper to taste

Topper/pat of butter and red bell
　pepper, diced small

- Combine the #1 ingredients in a large soup pot and bring to a simmer for 15 minutes, or until the green beans and peas are tender. Serve.

Goes well with *Spinach Loaf*, page 141.

Cantonese Vegetable Soup

about 6 16-ounce servings

#1 Ingredients
1 tablespoon toasted sesame seed oil
1/2 teaspoon fresh ginger, grated
1 cup onion, diced small
1/4 cup green bell pepper, diced small
1/2 cup carrots, diced small
1 cup celery, diced small
1 cup fresh mushrooms, sliced

10 small, fresh, and tender snow pods
1 6-ounce can sliced bamboo shoots, drained
1 6-ounce can sliced water chestnuts, drained
1 cup fresh broccoli florets, or 1 10-ounce package, frozen
white pepper to taste
1 tablespoon soy sauce

#2 Ingredients
6 cups chicken stock
1 cup fresh spinach, packed and chopped, or 1 10-ounce package, frozen

Topper/green onions, sliced

• Sauté the #1 ingredients until just tender. In a large soup pot combine the #1 and #2 ingredients, and bring to a simmer for 15 minutes. Serve.

Goes well with *Cheese and Onion Scones*, page 191.

Tofu Veggie Soup

about 7 16-ounce servings

#1 Ingredients
4 cups beef or chicken stock
1 cup celery, sliced thin
1 cup carrots, sliced thin
1 cup fresh mushrooms, sliced thin
1/2 cup turnip, peeled and diced small
1/4 cup bell pepper, diced small

2 14-ounce cans stewed tomatoes
1 10-ounce block extra firm tofu, diced
1/3 cup quick barley
1/2 cup cabbage, chopped

Topper/chives

• Combine the #1 ingredients in a large soup pot and bring to a simmer for 30 minutes. Serve.

Goes well with *Cheesy Onion Bread Sticks*, page 199.

Colonial Onion Soup

about 3 16-ounce servings

#1 Ingredients
1 tablespoon butter
1 cup onion, packed and thinly
   sliced

#2 Ingredients
1 pint half-and-half
4 cups milk

1/8 teaspoon ground nutmeg or
   to taste (optional)
2 egg yolks
salt and pepper to taste

Topper/you pick one!

- Mix the #2 ingredients with a wire whisk and set aside.
- In a large soup pot, sauté the #1 ingredients until onions are transparent. Add the #2 ingredients and bring to a simmer, stirring constantly until well heated and thickened. Serve.

Goes well with *Rye, Caraway and Cheese Bread Sticks,* page 199.

French Onion Soup

about 5 16-ounce servings

#1 Ingredients
4 cups onions, thinly sliced
   (in rings)
1 tablespoon butter or olive oil
salt and white pepper to taste

#2 Ingredient
6 cups beef stock

#3 Ingredients
6 thick slices crusty French bread
6 slices mozzarella cheese

- In a large soup pot, sauté the #1 ingredients until the onions are transparent. Add the #2 ingredient and bring to a simmer for 10 minutes.
- Serve the soup in individual oven-proof bowls and top with French bread and cheese. Put under the broiler until brown. Serve.

Salsa and Onion Soup

about 5 16-ounce servings

#1 Ingredients
2 cups chicken stock
4 cups chunky salsa, either mild, medium, or hot (optional)
1 cup onion, chopped
1/2 cup carrots, grated
1 cup celery, diced small
2 medium potatoes, peeled and diced small
1/2 cup frozen corn
1/2 cup frozen peas
3 tablespoons fresh cilantro, chopped
1 tablespoon fresh parsley, chopped
1/2 tablespoon liquid cayenne pepper or to taste
salt to taste

Topper/tortilla chips

• Combine the #1 ingredients in a large soup pot and bring to a simmer for 30 minutes. Serve.

Goes well with *Cheese and Cayenne Drop Biscuits, page 181.*

Onion and Tomato Soup

about 6 16-ounce servings

#1 Ingredients
4 cups chicken stock
1 cup onion, diced small
2 large tomatoes, chopped
1/2 cup carrots, grated
1/2 cup green onions, thinly sliced
1/4 cup fresh parsley, chopped
2 14-ounce cans stewed tomatoes
3 tablespoons fresh cilantro, chopped
salt and pepper to taste

#2 Ingredient
1/2 cup uncooked funghin-type pasta or any small, shaped pasta

#3 Ingredient
1/4 cup your favorite Italian salad dressing

Topper/Parmesan cheese and chives

• Cook, rinse, and drain the #2 ingredient and set aside. Combine all the #1 ingredients in a large soup pot and bring to a simmer for 20 minutes.
• Add the #2 ingredient and continue to simmer for another 5 minutes. Add the #3 ingredient, and reheat. Serve.

Goes well with *Tomato, Basil and Garlic Bread Sticks, page 199.*

Fresh Asparagus Soup

about 6 16-ounce servings

#1 Ingredients
4 cups chicken stock
1 cup leeks, sliced thin (whites
  only)
1 cup celery, sliced thin
1/2 cup carrots, grated
salt and pepper to taste
1/2 teaspoon fresh garlic, minced,
  or 1/4 teaspoon garlic powder

#2 Ingredient
1 pound fresh asparagus (tender
  parts only), sliced with the tops
  left whole

#3 Ingredient
1 cup uncooked angel-hair pasta,
  broken into 1-inch pieces

Topper/grated Parmesan cheese

- Combine the #1 ingredients in a large soup pot and bring to a simmer for 15 minutes. Add the #2 ingredient and continue to simmer another 5 minutes. Add the #3 ingredient, cook another 3 to 5 minutes, and serve.

Goes well with *Three Cheese Wine Bread*, page 143.

Hara Shorva

INDIA'S PEA SOUP

about 5 16-ounce servings

#1 Ingredients
6 cups chicken stock
2 cups potatoes, peeled and diced
  small
1 cup onion, diced small
1 teaspoon fresh ginger, grated
1/2 teaspoon coriander seeds,
  crushed (mash with the bottom
  of a glass on a hard surface)
2 teaspoons cumin seeds
5 tablespoons fresh coriander
  leaves, chopped

1 small hot chile (optional)
salt and pepper to taste

#2 Ingredients
1 10-ounce package frozen peas
salt and pepper to taste

#3 Ingredient
1 cup half-and-half

Topper/pat of butter and fresh
  lemon juice to taste

- Combine the #1 ingredients in a large soup pot and bring to a simmer for 15 minutes. Add the #2 ingredients and continue to simmer for another 15 minutes.
- Using a blender, blend until smooth, return to the heat, and slowly add the #3 ingredient, stirring constantly until reheated. Serve.

Goes well with *French Fried Onion Biscuits*, page 169.

Spinach Soup

about 3 16-ounce servings

#1 Ingredient
6 slices bacon, diced

#2 Ingredients
6 cups packed fresh spinach,
   chopped
1/2 cup onion, diced
1 cup leeks, sliced thin (whites
   only)
1 tablespoon butter or olive oil

#3 Ingredients
4 cups chicken stock
1/4 cup Italian dressing
salt and pepper to taste

Topper/chopped hard-boiled egg

• Brown and drain the #1 ingredient. Sauté the #2 ingredients. Combine the #1, #2, and #3 ingredients in a large soup pot and bring to a simmer for 20 minutes. Serve.

Goes well with *Sausage and Cheese Biscuits*, page 172.

Turkish Spinach Soup

about 4 16-ounce servings

#1 Ingredients
6 cups chicken stock
3 cups packed fresh spinach,
   chopped
1/2 cup carrots, grated
1/2 celery, sliced thin

1 tablespoon butter
1 tablespoon fresh dill weed
salt and pepper to taste

#2 Ingredients
2 eggs, beaten

• Combine the #1 ingredients in a large soup pot and bring to a simmer for 20 minutes. Slowly drizzle in the #2 ingredients and continue to simmer another 2 minutes. Serve.

Goes well with *Pepper Buttermilk Biscuits*, page 175.

Tomato Cabbage Soup

about 5 16-ounce servings

#1 Ingredients
2 cups beef stock
2 14-ounce cans stewed tomatoes
1 cup celery, chopped
1 cup onion, chopped
4 cups packed cabbage, shredded
1/2 teaspoon fresh oregano, or 1/4
 teaspoon, dried

1 teaspoon fresh thyme, chopped,
 or 1/2 teaspoon, dried
1 teaspoon fresh basil, chopped,
 or 1/2 teaspoon, dried
salt and pepper to taste

Topper/diced tomatoes with fresh
dill

• Combine the #1 ingredients in a large soup pot and bring to a simmer for
 30 minutes. Serve.

Goes well with *Mexican Corn Bread*, page 188.

Caraway and Cabbage Soup

about 6 16-ounce servings

#1 Ingredients
6 cups beef stock
6 cups packed cabbage, shredded
1 tablespoon tomato paste
1 tablespoon garlic, minced, or 1/2
 tablespoon garlic powder
1/2 cup onion, chopped
3 tablespoons sugar

1 tablespoon caraway seeds
salt and pepper to taste

#2 Ingredient
2 tablespoons lemon juice

Topper/Parmesan cheese

• Combine the #1 ingredients in a large soup pot and bring to a simmer for
 20 minutes. Add the #2 ingredient, give a good stir, and serve.

Goes well with *Pickle in a Loaf,* page 131.

Oriental Water Cress Soup

about 5 16-ounce servings

#1 Ingredient
10 medium-sized dried shiitake
   mushrooms

#2 Ingredients
6 cups chicken stock
2 large fresh bunches water cress,
   chopped, stems removed

1/2 cup fresh mushrooms, sliced
   thin
1/8 cup soy sauce
pepper to taste

Topper/green onion, thinly sliced

• Soak the #1 ingredient in hot water for 15 minutes and slice very thin. Combine the #1 and #2 ingredients in a large soup pot and bring to a simmer for 20 minutes. Serve.

Goes well with *Celery Seed Crackers*, page 200.

Escarole Soup

about 4 16-ounce servings

#1 Ingredients
6 cups chicken stock
6 cups packed fresh escarole,
   chopped
1/2 cup onion, diced small
1 teaspoon fresh garlic, minced,
   or 1/2 teaspoon garlic powder
salt and white pepper to taste

#2 Ingredient
1 egg, slightly beaten

Topper/grated Parmesan cheese

• Combine the #1 ingredients in a large soup pot and bring to a simmer for 10 minutes. Slowly drizzle the #2 ingredient into the #1 ingredients. Continue to simmer for another 1 to 2 minutes. Serve.

Goes well with *Garlic Crackers*, page 201.

Greens Soup

A FAVORITE DOWN SOUTH

about 6 16-ounce servings

#1 Ingredients
8 cups chicken stock
1 cup dried black-eyed peas
2 cups smoked ham, diced
1 cup onion, chopped

6 cups packed fresh collard
   greens, chopped
1 teaspoon fresh garlic, minced
salt and pepper to taste

Topper/diced red onions

- Combine the #1 ingredients in a large soup pot and bring to a simmer for 1 hour or until the peas are tender. Serve.

Goes well with *Quick Curry Bread*, page 127.

Borscht

about 4 16-ounce servings

#1 Ingredients
4 cups chicken stock
2 15-ounce cans shredded beets
   with the liquid

2 tablespoons light brown sugar
2 tablespoons lemon juice
1/8 teaspoon white pepper or to
   taste

Topper/big spoonful of sour
   cream

- Heat #1 ingredients until the sugar is melted. You can serve borscht either warm or cold.

Goes well with you pick one.

Variation: Use 6 medium fresh beets. Wash and trim the beets, leaving at least 2 inches of the stems. Cook the beets until tender, then peel and dice small. Use 2 cups of the beet water. You will need at least 2 cups of diced beets for this recipe, plus 1 extra tablespoon of brown sugar.

Goes well with *Onion Sage Bread*, page 130.

Have-To-Love-Okra Chowder

about 7 16-ounce servings

#1 Ingredients
6 cups chicken stock
1 10-ounce package frozen okra
1/2 cup carrots, grated
1 cup celery, sliced thin
1 large tomato, peeled and diced

1 cup onion, chopped small
2 14-ounce cans stewed tomatoes
salt and white pepper to taste

#2 Ingredient
1/2 cup uncooked minute rice

Topper/chives

- Combine the #1 ingredients in a large soup pot and bring to a simmer for 20 minutes or until the celery is tender. Add the #2 ingredient. Let set for 5 minutes and serve.

Goes well with *Onion and Dill Buttermilk Loaf*, page 136.

Portuguese Cucumber Soup

about 6 16-ounce servings

#1 Ingredients
6 cups chicken stock
3 large cucumbers, peeled,
    seeded, and diced small
4 large tomatoes, diced
1 cup red bell pepper, diced small
1/2 tablespoon fresh garlic, minced
1 cup onion, diced
salt and pepper to taste

#2 Ingredients
1/2 cup lemon juice
1 cup dry white wine

Topper/thinly sliced cucumber

- Combine the #1 ingredients in a large soup pot and bring to a simmer for 20 minutes. Add the #2 ingredients, continue to simmer for 10 more minutes, and serve.

Goes well with *Easy Popover*, page 196.

Chestnut Soup

about 5 16-ounce servings

#1 Ingredient
2 pounds raw fresh chestnuts

#2 Ingredients
4 cups chicken stock
2 tablespoons butter
1 cup carrots, grated
1/2 cup celery, diced small

1/4 cup onion, diced small
salt and white pepper to taste

#3 Ingredients
1 pint half-and-half
1 cup sour cream

Topper/toasted coconut

- Using a sharp knife cut an X on the flat side of each chestnut, cutting down to the meat of the nut. Place on a cookie sheet and bake at 450° for 10 to 15 minutes or until the shells crack open. Peel while still warm and set aside.

- Combine the #2 ingredients in a large soup pot and bring to a simmer for 20 minutes or until the veggies are tender. Mix the #3 ingredients together with a wire whisk and set aside. Using a blender, blend the #1 and #2 ingredients together, blending until smooth.

- Slowly add the #3 ingredients and blend until well mixed. Return to the heat, stirring constantly until reheated and serve.

Goes well with *Apple Fritters,* page 204.

Sweet Potato Soup

about 6 16-ounce servings

#1 Ingredients
6 cups beef stock
1 cup onion, chopped
1 cup celery, sliced thin
1 teaspoon fresh tarragon, or 1/2 teaspoon, dried (not ground)
1/8 teaspoon caraway seeds or to taste

1 tablespoon butter
1 cup carrots, grated
1 1/2 cups leeks, sliced (white part only)
4 cups sweet potatoes or yams, peeled and diced small

Topper/toasted sesame seeds

- Combine the #1 ingredients in a large soup pot and bring to a simmer for 30 minutes, or until the sweet potatoes are tender, and serve.

Goes well with *Spicy Hot Seedy Scones*, page 191.

Minestra di Riso e Basilico

BASIL AND RICE SOUP

about 5 16-ounce servings

#1 Ingredients
6 cups chicken stock
1 cup onion, diced small
1/2 cup carrots, grated
1 cup celery, diced small
1 cup fresh tomatoes, diced
4 tablespoons fresh basil,
    chopped, or 2 tablespoons
    dried flakes
salt and pepper to taste

#2 Ingredient
1/2 cup uncooked minute rice

Topper/grated Romano cheese

• Combine the #1 ingredients together in a large soup pot and bring to a simmer for 20 minutes. Add the #2 ingredient, wait 5 minutes and serve.

Goes well with *Tall Biscuits*, page 168.

Malaysian Lemony Rice Soup

about 4 16-ounce servings

#1 Ingredients
6 cups chicken stock
1 dried bay leaf
1/4 teaspoon fresh summer savory
    or 1/8 teaspoon dried flakes

#2 Ingredients
1/2 cup uncooked minute rice
salt and white pepper to taste
6 tablespoons fresh lemon juice

#3 Ingredient
4 beaten eggs

Topper/fresh lemon zest

• Combine the #1 ingredients in a large soup pot and bring to a simmer for 10 minutes. Add the #2 ingredients and continue to simmer for 5 minutes. Remove from heat, slowly drizzle in the #3 ingredient, and let sit 5 minutes. Serve.

Goes well with *Lemon Poppy Bread*, page 146.

Veggies with Basil and Vermicelli Soup

about 8 16-ounce servings

#1 Ingredients
6 cups chicken stock
1 cup onion, diced small
2 teaspoons fresh garlic,
   minced
1/2 cup carrots, sliced thin
1 cup celery, sliced thin
1 15-ounce can navy beans,
   rinsed and drained
1 cup red bell pepper, diced
1/2 cup frozen corn
1 cup fresh mushrooms, sliced

4 tablespoons fresh basil, chopped
1 cup fresh broccoli florets, or 1
   10-ounce frozen package,
   chopped
salt and pepper to taste

#2 Ingredient
2 cups uncooked vermicelli,
   broken into 1-inch pieces

Topper/shredded mozzarella
cheese with chives

• Combine all the #1 ingredients in a large soup pot and bring to a simmer
for 30 minutes. Add the #2 ingredient and continue to simmer for another
3 to 5 minutes, stirring frequently. Serve.

Goes well with *Parmesan Garlic Loaf*, page 142.

Italian Zucchini Soup with Macaroni

about 6 16-ounce servings

#1 Ingredients
4 cups chicken stock
2 cups fresh zucchini, thickly
   sliced
2 teaspoons garlic, minced
3 tablespoons fresh basil, diced
   small
1 cup onion, chopped
1/2 cup carrots, grated
1 cup celery, sliced thin

1/2 pound fresh mushrooms, sliced
2 14-ounce cans Italian stewed
   tomatoes
salt and pepper to taste

#2 Ingredient
1 cup uncooked shell macaroni

Topper/diced red and green
onions

• Combine the #1 ingredients in a large soup pot and bring to a simmer for
20 minutes. Add the #2 ingredient, and continue to simmer for 10 more
minutes. Serve.

Goes well with *Pepperoni and Cheese Biscuits*, page 172.

Broccoli Mushroom and Macaroni Soup

about 6 16-ounce servings

#1 Ingredients
6 cups chicken stock
2 cups fresh mushrooms, sliced
1 1/2 teaspoons fresh garlic,
    minced, or 3/4 teaspoon garlic
    powder
3 cups fresh broccoli florets or 1
    10-ounce package frozen
    chopped broccoli

1/2 cup onions, diced small
1/2 cup carrots, grated
salt and pepper to taste

#2 Ingredient
1 cup uncooked large elbow
    macaroni

Topper/grated Parmesan cheese

- Cook the #2 ingredient, drain, and set aside.
- Combine the #1 ingredients in a large soup pot and bring to a simmer for 15 minutes or until the broccoli is tender. Add the #2 ingredient, stir, and serve.

Goes well with *Carrot and Millet Loaf*, page 160.

Italian Bread Soup

MADE THE EASY WAY

about 4 16-ounce servings

#1 Ingredients
6 cups chicken stock
1 cup onion, chopped
1/2 cup celery, diced small
1 teaspoon garlic, minced, or 1/2
    teaspoon garlic powder
2 large tomatoes, chopped
1 small dried bay leaf
1 tablespoon fresh basil, chopped

1/4 cup fresh parsley, chopped
salt and pepper to taste

#2 Ingredient
box of your favorite croutons

Topper/grated Romano cheese
    and fresh chives

- Combine the #1 ingredients in a large soup pot and bring to a simmer for 30 minutes. Place croutons in each bowl, ladle the soup over them, and serve.

Goes well with *Pepperoni and Cheese Biscuits*, page 172.

Tomato with Macaroni Soup

about 4 16-ounce servings

#1 Ingredients
2 cups beef or chicken stock
2 14-ounce cans Italian stewed
  tomatoes
salt and pepper to taste

#2 Ingredient
1 cup uncooked large elbow
  macaroni

Topper/grated Parmesan and
  Romano cheese

• Combine the #1 ingredients in a large soup pot and bring to a simmer. Add
the #2 ingredient, continue to simmer for 10 minutes, and serve.

Goes well with *Bacon and Cheese Biscuits*, page 172.

Veggie Gumbo

about 8 16-ounce servings

#1 Ingredients
4 cups chicken stock
1/2 cup onion, chopped
1/2 cup celery, sliced
1/2 cup green bell pepper, diced
1/4 cup fresh parsley, chopped
1/2 cup frozen corn
1 14-ounce can black-eyed peas,
  drained
2 14-ounce cans stewed tomatoes
2 cups packed fresh spinach,
  chopped, or 1 10-ounce
  package frozen chopped
  spinach, defrosted
4 cups fresh okra, sliced, or 2
  10-ounce packages sliced or
  cut okra, defrosted
1/4 teaspoon cayenne pepper or to
  taste
1 teaspoon Old Bay seasoning
salt and pepper to taste

#2 Ingredient
2 tablespoons Worcestershire
  sauce

Topper/oyster crackers with fresh
  chives, sliced

• Combine the #1 ingredients in a large soup pot and bring to a simmer for
45 minutes. Add the #2 ingredients, give a good stir, and serve.

Goes well with *Wine and Cheese Bread*, page 143.

Chapter 3

MEATY SOUPS MADE WITH BEANS

- It is important that you rinse and pick over the beans to make sure there are no foreign objects like rocks and twigs.
- Beans need to be presoaked and cooked for the time given in the recipes. Soaking is not necessary for dried lentils or peas.
- To soak beans, cover with 1 to 2 inches of water. You can soak overnight for at least 8 hours. If you forget to soak, boil the beans in the required amount of water for 10 minutes, and let soak for one hour.
- The reason for soaking is the significant reduction in cooking time. When a recipe calls for several different kinds of beans you can soak them together.

1 cup of dried beans will yield about 3½ cups of cooked beans.

FOR 1 CUP DRIED BEANS	COOKING TIME, PRESOAKED BEANS
Black beans	1½ - 2 hours
Black-eyed peas	1½ - 2 hours
Garbanzo beans	2 - 3 hours
Great northern beans	1½ - 2 hours
Kidney beans	1½ - 2 hours
Lentils	45 minutes to 1 hour, unsoaked
Lima beans	1½ - 2 hours
Navy beans	1½ - 2 hours
Pinto beans	1½ - 2 hours
Split peas	45 minutes to 1 hour, unsoaked

- I have found adding salt or tomatoes makes no difference in the texture or digestibility of beans. However, if the packaged beans you have bought are old, you might end up with a tough bean dish, but I haven't found that too often.

Note: There are lots of suggestions on how to take the gas-causing effect out of beans and I've tried them all. I don't like the method of pouring off the water you soak the beans in or cook in, because that is where all the nutrients are. I have found something that does work most of the time: Peel a large potato and drop it down in the pot of cooking beans and remove in the first half of the cooking time. Believe me, you don't want to eat it or give it to the dog, just throw it away. The potato is not in any of the recipes for this purpose. Do try it, though.

Three Bean Soup

IF YOU LIKE BAKED BEANS, YOU'LL LIKE THIS ONE

about 8 16-ounce servings

#1 Ingredients
1 pound hamburger
8 slices bacon, diced
1 cup onion, chopped small

#2 Ingredients
8 cups beef stock
1/4 cup dried black beans, soaked
1/2 cup dried pinto beans, soaked
1/4 cup lima beans, soaked
1 tablespoon fresh basil, chopped

1 tablespoon fresh oregano,
   chopped
salt and pepper to taste

#3 Ingredients
1/2 cup catsup
1/2 cup packed brown sugar
3 tablespoons spicy mustard
2 tablespoons barbecue sauce

Topper/diced onions

• Brown and drain the #1 ingredients, and set aside.
• Mix the #3 ingredients with a wire whisk and set aside.

Combine the #2 ingredients in a large soup pot and bring to a simmer for 1 hour. Add the #1 ingredients and continue to simmer for 30 minutes. Add the #3 ingredients, stirring constantly until well blended. Continue to simmer for 10 minutes or until the brown sugar is melted. Serve.

Goes well with *Logan Bread*, page 165.

Ranch-Style Black Bean Soup

about 8 16-ounce servings

#1 Ingredients
6 cups chicken stock
2 cups smoked ham, diced
1 cup dried black beans, soaked
1 cup onions, chopped

2 teaspoons fresh garlic, minced
salt and pepper to taste

Topper/sour cream with chives

• Combine the #1 ingredients in a large soup pot and bring to a simmer for 1 1/2 hours or until the beans are tender. Serve.

Goes well with *Simple Biscuits*, page 167.

Cuban Black Bean Soup

about 8 16-ounce servings

#1 Ingredients
6 cups chicken stock
2 cups smoked ham, diced
1 cup dried black beans, soaked
1 cup onion, chopped
1 teaspoon fresh garlic, minced
1 cup bell pepper, chopped
2 cups tomatoes, chopped

1 teaspoon ground cumin
1 teaspoon fresh oregano,
    chopped
salt and pepper to taste

#2 Ingredient
¼ cup dark rum

Topper/diced onions

• Combine the #1 ingredients in a large soup pot and bring to a simmer for 1 hour, or until the beans are tender. Add the #2 ingredient, simmer 15 minutes, and serve.

Goes well with *Paraguay Corn Loaf*, page 189.

• See pages 32-34 for other recipes made with pork and beans.

Black Beans and Sausage with Cumin Soup

about 6 16-ounce servings

#1 Ingredients
6 cups chicken stock
1 15-ounce can black beans with
    liquid
2 cups kielbasa sausage, cut into
    bite-sized pieces
1 cup onion, chopped
⅔ cup green bell pepper,
    chopped

1 teaspoon garlic, minced
1 teaspoon ground cumin
1 tablespoon butter
salt and pepper to taste

Topper/sour cream with diced
    onion

• Combine the #1 ingredients in a large soup pot and bring to a simmer for 30 minutes. Serve.

Goes well with *Pepper Popovers*, page 197.

Calico Bean Soup

about 8 16-ounce servings

#1 Ingredients
6 cups chicken stock
1/8 cup each, soaked: dried black-eyed peas, dried navy beans, dried black beans
1/8 cup dried lentils
2 cups ham, cut into bite-sized pieces
2 14-ounce cans stewed tomatoes

1 teaspoon garlic, minced
1 cup onion, chopped
1/2 tablespoon chili powder or to taste
1 teaspoon ground cumin

Topper/sour cream with diced red onion

• Combine the #1 ingredients in a large soup pot and bring to a simmer for 1 1/2 hours or until the black beans are tender. Serve.

Goes well with *Salsa Loaf*, page 140.

Spanish Black Bean Soup

about 6 16-ounce servings

#1 Ingredients
6 cups chicken stock
1 cup dried black beans, soaked
1 teaspoon fresh garlic, minced
1 large dried bay leaf

#2 Ingredients
2 cups smoked ham, cut into bite-sized pieces
1/2 cup celery, sliced
1 cup yellow onion, chopped
1 tablespoon dry ground mustard

1 tablespoon chile powder or to taste
1 tablespoon butter
1 tablespoon liquid cayenne pepper or to taste (not tabasco)
salt to taste

#3 Ingredients
1 cup half-and-half
1 cup sour cream
1/4 cup lemon juice

Topper/thinly sliced lemons

• Mix the #3 ingredients together with a wire whisk and set aside.

• Combine the #1 ingredients in a large soup pot and bring to a simmer for 1 hour. Add the #2 ingredients and continue to simmer for another 30 minutes. Slowly add the #3 ingredients, stirring constantly until reheated. Serve.

Goes well with *Lemon Poppy Bread*, page 146.

Beef with Three Beans

about 7 16-ounce servings

#1 Ingredients
4 cups beef stock
2 cups stew beef, diced small
1 14-ounce can stewed tomatoes
1 cup onion, chopped
1 10-ounce package frozen lima
   beans, defrosted
1 15-ounce can butter beans,
   drained

1 15-ounce can kidney beans,
   drained
1 teaspoon fresh marjoram leaves,
   minced
1 teaspoon fresh thyme
salt and pepper to taste

Topper/sour cream with
   horseradish mixed in (to taste)

• Combine the #1 ingredients in a large soup pot and bring to a simmer for
45 minutes or until the meat is tender. Serve.

Goes well with *Monkey Bread*, page 155.

THYME

Garbanzo Bean Soup

about 6 16-ounce servings

#1 Ingredients
6 cups beef stock
1 15-ounce can garbanzo beans,
   drained
2 cups smoked ham, diced
1 cup onion, diced
1 teaspoon fresh garlic, minced
1/8 teaspoon cayenne pepper or to
   taste

1 cup potato, peeled and diced
1/2 cup celery, diced
1 cup tomatoes, diced
4 cups packed cabbage, shredded
salt to taste

Topper/Parmesan cheese

• Combine the #1 ingredients in a large soup pot and bring to a simmer for
45 minutes. Serve.

Goes well with *Tall Biscuits*, page 168.

Loaded Garbanzo Bean Soup

about 6 16-ounce servings

#1 Ingredient
1 pound mild sausage, ground

#2 Ingredients
6 cups chicken stock
1 15-ounce can garbanzo beans, drained
1 cup celery, diced small
1 cup packed cabbage, chopped

1/2 cup carrots, diced small
2 14-ounce cans stewed tomatoes
2 cups zucchini, sliced
1 teaspoon garlic, minced
1 tablespoon fresh basil, chopped
1/2 tablespoon fresh rosemary
salt and pepper to taste

Topper/Parmesan cheese

• Brown and drain the #1 ingredient. Combine the #1 and #2 ingredients together in a large soup pot, and bring to a simmer for 45 minutes. Serve.

Goes well with *Beer and Onion Fritters*, page 203.

Beef, Barley, and Lentils Soup

about 6 16-ounce servings

#1 Ingredients
4 cups beef stock
1/2 cup dried lentils
1 cup stew beef, cut into bite-sized pieces
1 cup leeks, sliced (whites only)
1/2 cup celery, sliced
1 cup zucchini, chopped
1/2 cup onion, chopped
1 teaspoon garlic, minced

1/2 cup quick cooking barley
2 14-ounce cans stewed tomatoes
1/4 cup fresh parsley, chopped
1/2 tablespoon fresh thyme, chopped
1 tablespoon fresh basil, chopped
salt and pepper to taste

Topper/sour cream and sliced black olives

• Combine the #1 ingredients in a large soup pot and bring to a simmer for 1 hour or until the lentils are tender. Serve.

Goes well with *Mustard and Chive Crackers*, page 201.

German Lentil Stew

about 8 16-ounce servings

#1 Ingredients
8 cups chicken stock
1 cup dried lentils
8 slices bacon, diced
2 cups smoked ham, cut into bite-
  sized pieces
1 cup onion, chopped
1/2 cup carrots, sliced
1/2 cup celery, sliced

1 small dried bay leaf
1 teaspoon fresh thyme, chopped
salt and pepper to taste

#2 Ingredient
juice from 2 lemons

Topper/sour cream with
  Parmesan cheese

• Combine the #1 ingredients in a large soup pot and bring to a simmer for 1 hour or until the lentils are tender. Add the #2 ingredient, give a good stir, and serve.

Goes well with *Quick Onion Rye with Caraway Seeds Bread*, page 159.

I-Love-Lentils Stew

about 4 16-ounce servings

#1 Ingredients
6 cups chicken stock
2 cups smoked sausage, cut into
  bite-sized pieces
1 cup dried lentils
1 cup leeks, sliced (white parts
  only)
1/2 cup carrots, diced small

1/2 cup celery, diced small
1 teaspoon fresh oregano, minced
1 small dried bay leaf
1 teaspoon ground cumin
2 14-ounce cans stewed tomatoes
salt and pepper to taste

Topper/melba rounds

• Combine the #1 ingredients in a large soup pot and bring to a simmer for 1 hour. Serve.

Goes well with *Poppy Seed and Buttermilk Biscuits*, page 174.

Italian Lentils

about 6 16-ounce servings

#1 Ingredient
1 pound hamburger

#2 Ingredients
6 cups beef stock
1 16-ounce jar or can of spaghetti
    sauce, or about 2 cups of
    homemade sauce
1 cup dried lentils
1 cup onion, chopped

#3 Ingredient
1 cup of your favorite macaroni,
    uncooked

Topper/a good sprinkle of
    Parmesan cheese

• Cook the #3 ingredient, rinse, drain, and set aside.
• Brown and drain the #1 ingredient. Combine the #1 and #2 ingredients in a large soup pot, and bring to a simmer for 1 hour or until the lentils are tender. Add the #3 ingredient, stir, and serve.

Goes well with *Italian Sesame Seed Bread Sticks*, page 199.

Mung Bean Soup

about 4 16-ounce servings

#1 Ingredients
6 cups chicken stock
1 cup dried mung beans, soaked
1/2 cup onion, diced small
1/4 teaspoon ground coriander
1/4 teaspoon ground turmeric
1 teaspoon liquid cayenne pepper
    or to taste
1/4 teaspoon cumin seeds
salt and pepper to taste

#2 Ingredient
2 cups chicken, cut into bite-sized
    pieces

#3 Ingredient
1/2 cup uncooked minute rice

Topper/sour cream with chives

• Combine the #1 ingredients in a large soup pot and bring to a simmer for 30 minutes. Add the #2 ingredient and continue to simmer for another 30 minutes. Add the #3 ingredient, wait 5 minutes, and serve.

Goes well with *Black Bread*, page 129.

Kenyan-Style Bean Stew

about 8 16-ounce servings

#1 Ingredient
1 pound ground pork

#2 Ingredients
1 cup onion, chopped
1/2 cup carrots, sliced
1 cup fresh corn, cut off the cob,
   or 1 cup, frozen
1 tablespoon ground paprika
1 15-ounce can navy beans with
   liquid

1/2 teaspoon curry
1 cup fresh okra, sliced, or 1 cup,
   frozen sliced
5 cup beef stock
1 teaspoon ground cayenne
   pepper or to taste
salt to taste

Topper/diced green bell pepper

* Brown and drain the #1 ingredient.
* Combine the #1 and #2 ingredients and bring to a simmer for 45 minutes.
  Serve.

Goes well with *Buttery Beer Bread with Herbs*, page 133.

Cajun White Bean Soup

about 8 16-ounce servings

#1 Ingredients
6 cups chicken stock
1 cup dried navy beans, soaked
2 cups smoked ham, diced small
1 cup onion, chopped
1 cup green bell pepper, chopped
1 cup celery, thinly sliced
1 teaspoon garlic, minced
1 teaspoon chili powder
salt and pepper to taste

#2 Ingredients
1 14-ounce can Cajun stewed
   tomatoes
1 teaspoon cumin ground
1 tablespoon liquid cayenne
   pepper or to taste

Topper/diced red onion

* Combine the #1 ingredients in a large soup pot and bring to a simmer
  for 2 hours, or until the beans are tender. Add the #2 ingredients to the
  #1 ingredients and let simmer for another 10 minutes. Serve.

Goes well with *Chili and Sour Cream Corn Bread*, page 187.

Hearty Pasta Fagioli

GRANDMA PEZZANITI TAUGHT ME A SHORT
CUT TO THIS CLASSIC ITALIAN DISH

about 6 16-ounce servings

#1 Ingredients
3 strips of bacon, diced
2 cups smoked ham, cut into bite-
   sized pieces
1/2 cup onion, diced small
3 tablespoons pepperoni, diced
   small
1 tablespoon olive oil
1 teaspoon garlic, minced
1/2 tablespoon fresh basil, minced
1 teaspoon fresh oregano, minced

#2 Ingredients
4 cups chicken stock
1 15-ounce can white navy beans,
   drained
2 14-ounce cans Italian stewed
   tomatoes
salt and pepper to taste

#3 Ingredient
1 cup uncooked large elbow
   macaroni

Topper/lots of grated Parmesan
and Romano cheese

- Cook, rinse, and drain the #3 ingredient and set aside.
- Sauté the #1 ingredients, add the #1 and #2 ingredients together in a large soup pot, and bring to a simmer for 45 minutes. Add the #3 ingredient, give a good stir, and serve.

Goes well with *Italian Sesame Seed Bread Sticks*, page 199.

Good Old Ham and Bean Soup

about 5 16-ounce servings

#1 Ingredients
1 cup dried navy beans, soaked
2 cups smoked ham, cut into bite-
   sized pieces
1 cup onion, chopped
2/3 cup celery, diced small

1/2 cup carrots, grated
2 cups water
6 cups chicken stock
salt and pepper to taste

Topper/diced onions

- Combine the #1 ingredients in a large soup pot and bring to a simmer for 1 hour, or until the beans are soft. Serve.

Goes well with *Dill and Mustard Drop Biscuits*, page 181.

Red Beans and Rice Soup

NEW ORLEANS STYLE

about 7 16-ounce servings

#1 Ingredients
6 cups chicken stock
2 cups smoked ham, diced small
1 15-ounce can red beans,
   drained
1 cup onion, chopped
1 teaspoon fresh garlic, minced
1/2 cup green onions, sliced
1/2 cup fresh parsley, chopped
2 large tomatoes, diced
1/4 teaspoon ground cayenne
   pepper, or to taste
1 teaspoon fresh oregano,
   minced, or 1/2 teaspoon dried
   oregano

1 teaspoon fresh thyme, chopped
1 large dried bay leaf
salt and pepper to taste

#2 Ingredients
1/4 cup apple cider vinegar
1 1/2 tablespoons Worcestershire
   sauce

#3 Ingredient
1/2 cup uncooked minute rice

Topper/sour cream with lots of
   fresh sliced chives

- Mix the #2 ingredients together and set aside.
- Combine the #1 ingredients in a large soup pot and bring to a simmer for 45 minutes. Add the #2 ingredients and stir. Add the #3 ingredients, wait 5 minutes, and serve.

Goes well with *Cheese and Cayenne Biscuits*, page 181.

Split Pea Soup with Dill

about 5 16-ounce servings

#1 Ingredients
6 cups chicken stock
1 cup dry split peas
1 small dried bay leaf
2 cups ham, diced small

3 tablespoons fresh dill weed, or 1
   1/2 tablespoon, dried
1 teaspoon fresh garlic, minced
salt and pepper to taste

Topper/sour cream and chives

- Bring the #1 ingredients to a simmer for 1 hour or until the peas are tender. Serve.

Goes well with *Alabama Rice Bread*, page 163.

Dutch Split Pea Soup

ERWTENSOEP

about 5 16-ounce servings

#1 Ingredients
8 cups chicken stock
1 cup smoked sausage, cut into
　bite-sized pieces
1 cup dried split peas
1 cup ham, diced
1 cup leeks, sliced (whites only)

1/2 cup celery, sliced
1 teaspoon fresh garlic, minced
1 tablespoon fresh savory leaves,
　minced
salt and pepper to taste

Topper/shredded Edam cheese

• Combine the #1 ingredients in a large soup pot and bring to a simmer for 1 hour or until the peas are tender. Serve.

Goes well with *Sesame and Onion Drop Biscuits*, page 181.

Gul Artsoppa

A SWEDISH SOUP

about 4 16-ounce servings

#1 Ingredients
8 cups chicken stock
1 cup dried yellow split peas
2 cups smoked ham, cut into bite-
　sized pieces
1/2 cup onion, chopped

2 tablespoons fresh marjoram
　leaves, minced, or 1
　tablespoon, dried
1/2 cup carrots, grated
1/2 cup celery, diced small
salt and pepper to taste

Topper/sour cream

• Combine the #1 ingredients in a large soup pot and bring to a simmer for 1 hour or until the peas are soft. Serve.

Goes well with *Blue Corn Crackers*, page 200.

Chapter 4

MEATLESS SOUPS MADE WITH BEANS

Vegetable soup stock can be used instead of chicken or beef stock. See *Chapter 2* for instructions on preparing, soaking, and cooking beans.

Veggie Bean Soup

about 6 16-ounce servings

#1 Ingredients
6 cups chicken stock
2 15-ounce cans navy beans,
   rinsed and drained
1 cup leeks, thinly sliced (whites
   only)
1/2 cup carrots, grated
1/2 cup celery, sliced
1 cup fresh corn, cut off the cob,
   or 1 cup, frozen

1/2 cup green bell pepper, diced
1 small dried bay leaf
1 teaspoon fresh thyme, minced
salt and pepper to taste

#2 Ingredient
1 tablespoon Worcestershire sauce

Topper/diced red onion

• Combine the #1 ingredients in a large soup pot and bring to a simmer for 30 minutes, or until the celery is tender. Add the #2 ingredient, give a good stir, and serve.

Goes well with *Alabama Rice Bread*, page 163.

Curry and Black Bean Soup

about 8 16-ounce servings

#1 Ingredients
6 cups chicken stock
1 cup dry black beans, soaked
1 teaspoon fresh garlic, minced
1 cup onion, chopped
1/2 cup green bell pepper,
   chopped

3 tablespoons Worcestershire sauce
1 large dried bay leaf
1 teaspoon ground cumin
1 tablespoon curry powder
salt and pepper to taste

Topper/sour cream with diced
   red onion

• Combine the #1 ingredients in a large soup pot and bring to a simmer for 1 hour or until the beans are tender. Serve.

Goes well with *Chopped Broccoli and Cheese Corn Bread*, page 186.

Pasta and Bean Soup

about 6 16-ounce servings

#1 Ingredients
4 cups beef stock
1 15-ounce can navy beans, with
  liquid
1 cup onion, chopped
1 cup celery, diced small
1/2 cup carrots, grated
1 14-ounce can stewed tomatoes
1 tablespoon fresh garlic, minced
1 teaspoon fresh oregano,
  chopped

1/2 tablespoon tomato paste
2 teaspoons sugar
salt and pepper to taste

#2 Ingredient
1 cup uncooked large-shell
  macaroni

Topper/Parmesan cheese with
  fresh chives

- Cook, drain, and rinse the #2 ingredient, and set aside.
- Combine the #1 ingredients in a large soup pot and bring to a simmer for 20 minutes. Add the #2 ingredient, give a good stir, and serve.

Goes well with *Madeira Bread*, page 155.

Ful Nabed

AN EGYPTIAN SOUP

about 5 16-ounce servings

#1 Ingredient
1 15-ounce can white navy beans
  with liquid

#2 Ingredients
6 cups chicken stock
1 15-ounce can white navy beans,
  drained

1 cup onion, chopped
5 tablespoons fresh parsley
juice of 1 large lemon
salt and pepper to taste

Topper/lemon, thinly sliced

- Mash #1 ingredient with a fork and set aside (with the liquid).
- Combine the #2 ingredients in a large soup pot and bring to a simmer for 45 minutes. Add the #1 ingredient, stirring constantly until reheated. Serve.

Goes well with *Monkey Bread*, page 155.

Two-Bean Soup

about 4 16-ounce servings

#1 Ingredients
8 cups beef stock
1/2 cup black beans, soaked
1/2 cup pinto beans, soaked
2 tablespoons soy sauce
1 cup onion, chopped
1 tablespoon chili powder
1 teaspoon cumin seeds
1 1/2 teaspoons fresh oregano,
    chopped
2 tablespoons fresh cilantro,
    chopped
salt and pepper to taste

#2 Ingredient
1/2 cup fresh lime juice (or bottled)

#3 Ingredient
1 cup uncooked large-shell pasta

Topper/sour cream and chives

• Combine the #1 ingredients in a large soup pot and bring to a simmer for
  1 1/2 hours, or until the beans are tender. Add the #2 ingredient, give a quick
  stir, and serve.

Goes well with *Wheat Germ and Buttermilk Biscuits with Whole Wheat*,
page 174.

Quick Black Bean and Macaroni Soup

about 6 16-ounce servings

#1 Ingredients
4 cups beef stock
1 15-ounce can black beans,
    rinsed and drained
1/2 cup onion, chopped
1 cup zucchini, diced
1/2 cup fresh corn, cut off the cob,
    or 1/2 cup, frozen
1/2 cup frozen peas
2 14-ounce cans stewed tomatoes
salt and pepper to taste

#2 Ingredient
1 cup large elbow macaroni,
    uncooked

Topper/Parmesan cheese, grated

• Combine the #1 ingredients in a large soup pot and bring to a simmer for
  45 minutes. Add the #2 ingredient and continue to simmer for another 15
  minutes. Serve.

Goes well with *Sesame Seed Bread*, page 136.

A Favorite Navy Bean Soup

about 3 16-ounce servings

#1 Ingredients
1/2 cup onion, diced small
1/2 cup green bell pepper,
    chopped
1 tablespoon butter

#2 Ingredients
2 cups chicken stock
2 15-ounce cans navy beans
salt and pepper to taste

#3 Ingredient
1 tablespoon vinegar

Topper/chopped onion

- Sauté the #1 ingredients. Combine with the #2 ingredients in a large soup pot, and bring to a simmer for 20 minutes. Add the #3 ingredient, give a good stir, and serve.

Goes well with *Garlic and Mozzarella Cheese Drop Biscuits*, page 181.

Bunch of Beans Soup

about 6 16-ounce servings

#1 Ingredients
8 cups chicken stock
1 tablespoon each, soaked
    together: dried navy beans,
    pinto beans, black beans,
    garbanzo beans, lima beans,
    black-eyed peas
1 cup onion, chopped
1 cup carrots, sliced thin
1 cup celery, sliced thin
1 small dried bay leaf

#2 Ingredients
1 tablespoon each, dried: lentils,
    yellow split peas
1 teaspoon chili powder
1 teaspoon cumin
salt and pepper to taste

#3 Ingredient
1 14-ounce can stewed tomatoes

Topper/sour cream with chives

- Combine the #1 ingredients in a large soup pot and bring to a simmer for 45 minutes. Add the #2 ingredients and continue to simmer for another 45 minutes, watching to make sure you don't need to add more liquid. Add the #3 ingredient and continue to simmer for another 30 minutes, or until the garbanzo beans are tender. Serve.

Goes well with *Chives and Cheese Popovers*, page 197.

Khatte Chhole

AN INDIAN SOUR CHICKPEA SOUP MADE FAST AND EASY

about 6 16-ounce servings

#1 Ingredients
6 cups chicken stock
2 15-ounce cans chickpeas
(garbanzo beans), drained
1 cup onion, chopped
1 3-ounce can green chilies,
chopped
1 teaspoon fresh ginger, minced
1 cup tomatoes, chopped
1 teaspoon coriander seeds
1 teaspoon cumin seeds
1/2 teaspoon turmeric
1/4 teaspoon cayenne pepper or to
taste

#2 Ingredients
1/8 teaspoon each of the following
(ground): cardamom seeds,
cumin, cloves, black pepper,
nutmeg
juice of 2 lemons

Topper/thinly sliced lemons

• Combine the #1 ingredients in a large soup pot and bring to a simmer
for 1 hour. Stir in the #2 ingredients, continue to simmer for another 10
minutes, and serve.

Goes well with *Pepper Flat Bread*, page 208.

Yellow Split Pea Soup

about 4 16-ounce servings

#1 Ingredients
8 cups chicken stock
1 cup dry, yellow split peas
1/2 cup celery, chopped
1 teaspoon cumin

1/4 cup fresh parsley, chopped
1 teaspoon fresh garlic, minced
salt and pepper to taste

Topper/thinly sliced Edam cheese

• Combine the #1 ingredients in a large soup pot and bring to a simmer for
45 to 50 minutes or until the peas are soft. Serve.

Goes well with *Ham and Cheese Biscuits*, page 172.

Black Beans and Split Pea Soup

THIS IS A WINNING COMBINATION

about 5 16-ounce servings

#1 Ingredients
8 cups chicken stock
1/2 cup dried black beans, soaked
1/2 cup dried split peas
1/2 cup long-cooking barley
3 tablespoons tamari sauce
salt and pepper to taste

#2 Ingredients
1 cup packed fresh spinach,
  chopped
1 cup packed fresh kale, chopped
  and packed (optional)

Topper/sour cream with chives
  and dill weed

- Combine the #1 ingredients in a large soup pot and bring to a simmer for 1 hour. Add the #2 ingredients and simmer another 30 minutes, or until the beans are tender. Serve.

Goes well with *Native American Buckskin Bread*, page 207.

Indian Split Peas with Curry

about 6 16-ounce servings

#1 Ingredients
8 cups chicken stock
1 cup dried split peas
2 cups chicken, cut into bite-sized
  pieces

1/2 cup onion, diced small
1 teaspoon curry powder
salt and pepper to taste

Topper/toasted coconut

- Combine the #1 ingredients in a large soup pot and bring to a simmer for 1 hour or until the peas are soft. Serve.

Goes well with *Chapati Indian Flat Bread*, page 206.

Mongol Soup

about 5 16-ounce servings

#1 Ingredients
8 cups chicken stock
1 cup dried split peas

#2 Ingredients
1 14-ounce can stewed tomatoes
salt and pepper to taste

#3 Ingredients
1 pint half-and-half
2 teaspoons Worcestershire sauce
1/2 cup sherry
1 1/2 tablespoons sugar

Topper/your favorite crackers

- Mix the #3 ingredients together with a wire whisk and set aside.
- Combine the #1 ingredients in a large soup pot and bring to a simmer for 45 minutes or until the peas are tender. Add the #2 ingredients and continue to simmer for another 10 minutes. Slowly add the #3 ingredients, stirring constantly until reheated and serve.

Goes well with *Ginger and Banana Loaf*, page 154.

Crescenti Lentil Soup

about 6 16-ounce servings

#1 Ingredients
8 cups beef stock
1 cup dry lentils
1 cup carrots, diced small
2 cups potatoes, peeled and diced
   small
1 cup onion, diced small
1/2 cup celery, diced small
4 tablespoons celery leaves,
   chopped
1 1/2 cups tomatoes, diced small
1/2 teaspoon fresh marjoram,
   chopped
1/4 teaspoon pepper
2 cups zucchini, chopped
4 cups packed cabbage, shredded
salt and pepper to taste

Topper/shredded cheddar cheese

- Combine the #1 ingredients in a large soup pot and bring to a simmer for 1 hour, or until the lentils are tender. Serve.

Goes well with *Confetti Casserole Bread*, page 132.

Dal

A SOUP FROM INDIA, THE SHORT VERSION

about 4 16-ounce servings

#1 Ingredients
8 cups chicken stock
1½ cups dry lentils
¼ teaspoon ground turmeric
½ teaspoon ground cumin
½ teaspoon ground cardamom
1 cup onion, diced small

1 tablespoon butter
salt and pepper to taste

#2 Ingredient
juice of one lime

Topper/lime, thinly sliced

- Combine the #1 ingredients in a large soup pot and bring to a simmer for 1 hour. Using a blender, blend until smooth. Add the #2 ingredient, give a good stir, and reheat if needed. Serve.

Goes well with *Chapati Indian Flat Bread*, page 206.

Masoor Dal Soup

about 4 16-ounce servings

#1 Ingredients
8 cups chicken stock
1 cup dry lentils
¼ teaspoon fresh ginger, grated
½ teaspoon ground turmeric
1 teaspoon ground coriander
¼ teaspoon ground cayenne
    pepper

1 teaspoon whole cumin seeds
3 tablespoons coriander leaves,
    chopped
salt and white pepper to taste

Topper/plain yogurt with fresh
    chopped mint leaves

- Combine the #1 ingredients together in a large soup pot and bring to a simmer for 1 hour or until the lentils are tender. Serve.

Goes well with *Chapati Indian Flat Bread*, page 206.

Another Veggie and Lentil Soup from the Middle East

about 5 16-ounce servings

#1 Ingredients
6 cups chicken stock
1 cup lentils, dried
1/2 cup carrots, diced
1/2 cup celery, diced small
1 teaspoon garlic, minced
2 14-ounce cans stewed tomatoes
1 teaspoon cumin seeds
1/2 teaspoon allspice

3 cinnamon sticks
3 tablespoons fresh cilantro,
    chopped
salt and pepper to taste

#2 Ingredient
1 cup dry red wine

Topper/sour cream with mint leaves

• Combine the #1 ingredients in a large soup pot and bring to a simmer for
  1 hour or until the lentils are tender. Add the #2 ingredient and continue to
  simmer for 10 minutes. Remove cinnamon sticks and serve.

Goes well with *Onion and Parmesan Buttermilk Biscuits*, page 178.

African Lentils and Vegetable Stew

about 6 16-ounce servings

#1 Ingredients
6 cups chicken stock
1 1/2 cups dried lentils
1 cup onion, coarsely chopped
5 tablespoons fresh parsley,
    chopped
1 teaspoon garlic, minced
1 teaspoon ground cinnamon
1/2 teaspoon ground turmeric
1/2 teaspoon ground pepper

1/4 teaspoon ground ginger
1/2 cup carrots, diced
1 14-ounce can stewed tomatoes
1/2 cup fresh, shelled peas, or 1
    cup, frozen
1/2 cup fresh, green beans, cut, or
    1 cup, frozen
salt and pepper to taste

Topper/thinly sliced cucumber

• Combine the #1 ingredients in a large soup pot and bring to a simmer for
  1 hour, or until the lentils are tender. Serve.

Goes well with *Celery-Poppy Seed-Onion Bread*, page 129.

Cucumber and Mung Bean Soup

ANOTHER INDIAN DELICACY

about 4 16-ounce servings

#1 Ingredients

6 cups chicken stock
3/4 cup yellow mung bean, soaked
1/8 teaspoon ground turmeric
1/2 cup onion, diced small
3/4 teaspoon cumin seeds
2 teaspoons fresh coriander
    leaves, minced
salt and white pepper to taste

#2 Ingredients

3/4 cup potatoes, peeled, and
    grated
2 cups cucumber, peeled, seeded,
    and finely diced

Topper/thinly sliced lime

- Combine #1 ingredients in a large soup pot and bring to a simmer for 1 hour, or until the mung beans are tender.
- Add the #2 ingredients and continue to simmer for another 10 minutes. Using a blender, blend until smooth, reheat if need be and serve.

Goes well with *Chapati Indian Flat Bread*, page 206.

Chapter 5

SOUPS MADE WITH CHICKEN

Good Old Chicken and Rice
about 6 16-ounce servings

#1 Ingredients
6 cups chicken stock
2 cups chicken, cut into bite-sized
  pieces
1 cup onion, chopped
½ cup celery, sliced
½ cup carrots, sliced

4 cup fresh parley, chopped
salt and pepper to taste

#2 Ingredient
½ cup uncooked minute rice

Topper/your favorite crackers

• Combine the #1 ingredients in a large soup pot and bring to a simmer for
  45 minutes. Add the #2 ingredient, wait 5 minutes, and serve.

Goes well with *Corn Fritters*, page 202.

Chicken and Rotelle Pasta
about 7 16-ounce servings

#1 Ingredients
6 cups chicken stock
2 cups chicken, cut into bite-sized
  pieces
½ cup onion, chopped
½ cup celery, diced small
½ cup carrot, grated
2 cups fresh spinach, packed, or 1
  10-ounce package frozen
  spinach, defrosted (with the
  water squeezed out)
½ cup frozen corn
1 14-ounce can stewed tomatoes

1 small dried bay leaf
1 teaspoon fresh oregano, or ½
  teaspoon dried flakes
1 teaspoon fresh garlic, minced
1 tablespoon fresh basil, chopped
¼ cup fresh parsley, chopped
salt and pepper to taste

#2 Ingredient
1 cup uncooked rotelle pasta

Topper/Romano and Parmesan
  cheese, grated

• Cook and drain the #2 ingredient and set aside.
• Combine the #1 ingredients in a large soup pot and bring to a simmer for
  30 minutes. Add the #2 ingredient, and serve.

Goes well with *Garlic Loaf*, page 127.

Chicken Tortellini Soup

about 7 16-ounce servings

#1 Ingredients
4 cups chicken stock
2 cups chicken, cut into bite-sized
   pieces
1/2 cup carrots, sliced
1/2 cup celery, sliced
1/2 onion, chopped
2 cups fresh mushrooms, sliced
1 14-ounce can stewed tomatoes
1 teaspoon fresh garlic, minced

1/2 teaspoon ground cumin
1 15-ounce can kidney beans,
   drained
salt and pepper to taste

#2 Ingredient
2 cups uncooked tortellini

Topper/diced avocado with
   Parmesan cheese

• Combine the #1 ingredients in a large soup pot and bring to a simmer for 30 minutes, or until the veggies are tender. Add the #2 ingredient and let simmer for another 10 minutes. Serve.

Goes well with *Italian Sesame Seed Bread Sticks,,* page 199.

Chicken and Dill Soup

about 6 16-ounce servings

#1 Ingredients
6 cups chicken stock
2 cups chicken, cut into bite-sized
   pieces
2 cups potatoes, peeled and diced
   small
1/2 cup celery, sliced thin

1/2 cup onion, diced small
1 cup frozen corn
2 tablespoons fresh dill weed
2 tomatoes, chopped
1 small dried bay leaf
salt and pepper to taste

Topper/you pick one!

• Combine the #1 ingredients together in a large soup pot and bring to a simmer for 45 minutes. Serve.

Goes well with *Onion and Parmesan Buttermilk Biscuits,* page 178.

Chicken and Asparagus

about 6 16-ounce servings

#1 Ingredients
4 cups chicken stock
2 cups chicken, diced small
1 cup onion, diced small
1 cup celery, sliced thin
salt and pepper to taste

#2 Ingredient
2 cups tender parts of the
   asparagus, cut into bite-sized
   pieces

#3 Ingredients
1 teaspoon spicy mustard
1/2 teaspoon Worcestershire sauce
3/4 cup mashed potatoes or instant
   mashed potatoes
1 pint half-and-half

Topper/Parmesan cheese and
   fresh chives

- Mix the #3 ingredients together with a wire whisk and set aside. Combine the #1 ingredients together in a large soup pot and bring to a simmer for 20 minutes.
- Add the #2 ingredient, and continue to simmer for another 10 minutes. Add the #3 ingredients, stirring constantly and gently until well blended and heated through. Serve.

Goes well with *Sharp Cheddar Quick Bread*, page 138.

Classic Jewish Chicken Soup

THE EASY VERSION

about 6 16-ounce servings

#1 Ingredients
6 cups chicken stock
2 cups chicken, cut into bite-sized
   pieces
1 cup onion, chopped
1 cup celery, sliced thin
1 cup carrots, sliced thin

1/4 cup parsley, chopped
2 cups long-cooking soup noodles
salt and pepper to taste

Topper/diced tomatoes and
   croutons

- Combine the #1 ingredients together in a large soup pot and bring to a simmer for 30 minutes. Serve.

Goes well with *Herb and Onion Loaf,* page 131.

Matzo Ball Soup

about 5 16-ounce servings

#1 Ingredient
1 5-ounce package of matzo meal (you can find this in the ethnic section of your grocery store). This will make about 12 matzo balls. Just follow the package directions.

#2 Ingredients
1/2 cup onion, diced small
1/2 cup carrots, grated
1/8 teaspoon celery seed
8 cups chicken stock
salt and pepper to taste

Topper/sliced green onions

- Prepare the matzo balls and chill for one hour.
- Add the #2 ingredients to a large soup pot and bring to a simmer for 15 minutes. Add the #1 ingredient, and continue to simmer for another 20 minutes. Serve.

Cock-A-Leekie Soup

A SCOTTISH SOUP

about 5 16-ounce servings

#1 Ingredient
8 slices of bacon, diced

#2 Ingredients
6 cups chicken stock
2 cups chicken, cut into bite-sized pieces
1 small dried bay leaf
1/2 cup quick cooking barley
1 1/2 cups leeks, sliced (whites part only)
2 tablespoons fresh thyme, chopped
1/8 cup fresh parsley, chopped
1/2 cup carrots, grated
1/2 cup celery, diced small
salt and pepper to taste

Topper/Parmesan cheese

- Cook the #1 ingredient until slightly brown, and drain. Combine the #1 and the #2 ingredients in a large soup pot and bring to a simmer for 45 minutes, or until veggies are tender. Serve.

Goes well with *Lemon Pepper Crackers*, page 201.

Mulligatawny Soup

about 6 16-ounce servings

#1 Ingredients
6 slices bacon, diced
2 cups chicken, cut into bite-sized
    pieces
1/2 cup carrots, thinly sliced
1/2 cup celery, thinly sliced
1/2 teaspoon curry powder
6 peppercorns
3 whole cloves
1 large dried bay leaf

1/4 cup fresh parsley, chopped
2 cups Granny Smith apples,
    peeled and diced
6 cups chicken stock
salt and pepper to taste

#2 Ingredient
1 pint half-and-half

Topper/croutons and bacon bits

- Combine the #1 ingredients in a large soup pot and bring to a simmer for 45 minutes. Slowly add the #2 ingredient, stirring constantly until reheated. Serve.

Goes well with *Poppy Seed and Buttermilk Biscuits*, page 174.

Pam's Christmas Mexican Corn Chowder

about 8 16-ounce servings

#1 Ingredients
4 cups chicken, cut into bite-sized
    pieces
1/2 onion, chopped
2 teaspoons garlic, minced
1 medium tomato, chopped
3 tablespoons butter
1 15-ounce can cream-style corn
1 4-ounce can chopped green
    chilies, drained
1 teaspoon liquid cayenne pepper
2 tablespoons fresh cilantro,
    chopped

1 teaspoon ground cumin
6 cups chicken stock
salt and pepper to taste

#2 Ingredients
1 pint half-and-half
1 cup sour cream
2 cups Monterey Jack cheese,
    shredded

Topper/Monterey Jack,
    shredded, and fresh cilantro,
    chopped

- Mix the #2 ingredients together with a fork and set aside. Combine the #1 ingredients together in a large soup pot and bring to a simmer for 45 minutes. Slowly add the #2 ingredients, stirring constantly until the cheese melts. Serve.

Goes well with *Philly Poppy Seed Loaf*, page 137.

Tijuana Soup

about 8 16-ounce servings

#1 Ingredients
3 cups chicken, cut into bite-sized
  pieces
1 cup onion, chopped
1 tablespoon garlic, minced
1 cup potatoes, peeled and cut
  into bite-sized pieces
1/2 cup carrots, sliced
1/2 cup celery, sliced
1/2 cup red bell pepper, chopped
1 tablespoon fresh thyme, minced
1 teaspoon ground cumin
1 teaspoon fresh rubbed sage (rub
  it with your fingers to release
  the flavor), chopped

1 small dried bay leaf
liquid cayenne pepper to taste
3 tablespoon fresh cilantro,
  minced
6 cups chicken stock
salt and pepper to taste

#2 Ingredients
3 cups jalapeño cheese, shredded,
  or a cheese of your choice
1 cup half-and-half
1 cup sour cream

Topper/crushed tortilla chips with
  salsa on top

- Mix the #2 ingredients with a fork and set aside.
- Combine the #1 ingredients in a large soup pot and bring to a simmer for
  30 minutes, or until the veggies are tender. Slowly add the #2 ingredients to
  the #1 ingredients, stirring constantly until the cheese is melted. Serve.

Goes well with *Frito Corn Bread*, page 187.

Mexican Lime Soup

about 4 16-ounce servings

#1 Ingredients
1 cup chicken, cut into bite-sized
  pieces
1/2 cup chicken livers, chopped
1/2 cup chicken gizzards,
  chopped
1 cup onion, chopped
2 cups tomatoes, chopped
1/2 cup bell pepper, chopped
1 teaspoon oregano

6 cups chicken stock
salt and pepper to taste

#2 Ingredients
juice from 2 grapefruits
juice from 2 limes

Topper/place a few tortilla chips
  in the bottom of your bowl and
  pour the soup over them.

- Combine the #1 ingredients in a large soup pot and bring to a simmer for
  45 minutes. Add the #2 ingredients, give a good stir, and serve.

Goes well with *Basic Drop Biscuits*, page 181.

Chinese Noodle Soup

about 7 16-ounce servings

#1 Ingredients
2 cups chicken, cut into bite-sized
　　pieces
1 cup fresh mushrooms, sliced
1 cup carrots, grated
1 cup celery, diced small
1 teaspoon fresh ginger root,
　　minced
1 teaspoon garlic, minced
1 teaspoon sesame oil
1/2 cup dry white wine
2 tablespoons soy sauce
2 tablespoons sugar

6 cups chicken stock
pepper to taste

#2 Ingredient
2 packages ramen (oriental
　　noodles)

#3 Ingredient
2 1-ounce envelopes chicken
　　gravy mix

Topper/fried noodles with green
　　onions, sliced

- Cook the #3 ingredient, drain, and set aside.
- Combine the #1 ingredients in a large soup pot and bring to a simmer for 45 minutes.
- Prepare the #3 ingredient according to package directions, stir into the #1 ingredients, and add the #2 ingredient. Give a good stir and serve.

Goes well with *Tsung Yu Ping Flat Bread Chinese Onion Circles*, page 208.

Hot and Sour Soup

about 6 16-ounce servings

#1 Ingredients
2 cups chicken, diced small
4 fresh shiitake mushrooms, diced
1/2 cup rice vinegar
1/4 cup fresh bamboo shoots, peeled
　　and cut into julienne strips
2 tablespoons soy sauce
1 tablespoon fresh cilantro, chopped

1 1/2 teaspoons hot pepper sauce
　　(liquid cayenne pepper)
2 green onions, thinly sliced
6 cups chicken stock
pepper to taste

#2 Ingredient
1 egg, lightly beaten

- Combine the #1 ingredients in a large soup pot and bring to a simmer for 45 minutes. Slowly drizzle in the #2 ingredient and continue to simmer for another 1 to 2 minutes. Serve.

Goes well with *Sweet Little Honey Puffs*, page 205.

Variation: You may use other mushrooms if you can't find shiitake mushrooms.

Miso Soup

THIS IS A PERFECT START TO A JAPANESE-STYLE MEAL

about 5 16-ounce servings

#1 Ingredient
1 cup seaweed (wakame dry,
 found in Asian grocery stores)

#2 Ingredients
2 cups chicken, cut into bite-sized
 pieces
1/2 cup carrots, grated
1/2 cup celery, diced small

1 6-ounce can sliced water
 chestnuts, drained
4 tablespoons miso (soy bean paste)
3 scallions, thinly sliced
1 tablespoon soy sauce
6 cups chicken stock
white pepper to taste

Topper/sliced green onions with
 toasted sesame seeds

- Soak the #1 ingredient for 15 minutes and wash to get all the salt out.
- Combine the #1 and #2 ingredients in a large soup pot and bring to a simmer for 20 minutes. Serve.

Goes well with *Sesame Seed Crackers*, page 201.

A Soup from the Caribbean

about 7 16-ounce servings

#1 Ingredients
2 cups chicken, cut into bite-sized
 pieces
1/2 cup carrots, diced
1 cup onion, diced
1/2 cup green bell pepper, diced
1/2 cup red bell pepper, diced
1 cup zucchini, diced
2 cups tomatoes, diced
1/2 cup frozen corn
1/4 teaspoon paprika
1 teaspoon chili powder
1 teaspoon ground cumin

1 teaspoon fresh thyme, chopped
1/2 teaspoon curry powder
1/2 teaspoon ground turmeric
1 teaspoon fresh oregano, or 1/2
 teaspoon dried oregano flakes
6 cups chicken stock
salt and pepper to taste

#2 Ingredient
3 bananas, sliced

Topper/diced avocado

- Combine the #1 ingredients together in a large soup pot and bring to a simmer for 1 hour. Put a serving of the #2 ingredient in each bowl. Ladle soup over the bananas and serve.

Goes well with *Olive and Cream Cheese Loaf*, page 135.

Hamund Soup

EGYPTIAN SOUP WITH CHICKEN AND LEMON

about 5 16-ounce servings

#1 Ingredients
2 cups chicken, cut into bite-sized
  pieces
1 tablespoon butter
1/2 cup celery, diced small
1 cup leeks, sliced thin (white part
  only)
1 teaspoon garlic, minced
6 cups chicken stock
salt and pepper to taste

#2 Ingredient
1/2 cup minute rice

#3 Ingredient
juice of 2 lemons

Topper/grated Romano cheese

• Combine all the #1 ingredients in a large soup pot and bring to a simmer for 45 minutes. Add the #3 ingredient and stir. Add the #2 ingredient, wait 5 minutes, and serve.

Goes well with *Lemony Golden Raisin Bread*, page 145.

Hunter Chicken Stew

about 6 16-ounce servings

#1 Ingredients
2 cups chicken, cut into bite-sized
  pieces
1 teaspoon garlic, minced
1 teaspoon cinnamon powder
1 cup onion, chopped
1 cup celery, sliced thin
1/2 pound fresh mushrooms, sliced
2 14-ounce cans stewed tomatoes

1 cup dry sherry
4 cups chicken stock
salt and pepper to taste

#2 Ingredient
1 cup uncooked vermicelli pasta

Topper/sour cream with diced
  onion

• Combine all the #1 ingredients into a large soup pot and bring to a simmer for 30 minutes. Add the #2 ingredient and simmer another 10 minutes. Serve.

Goes well with *Spinach Loaf with Cheese*, page 141.

Brunswick Stew

about 7 16-ounce servings

#1 Ingredients
1 cup chicken, cut into bite-sized pieces
1 cup pork meat, cut into bite-sized pieces
1/2 cup onion, chopped
1/2 tablespoon butter

#2 Ingredients
1 14-ounce can stewed tomatoes
1 15-ounce can cream-style corn

1 10-ounce package frozen lima beans
1/2 teaspoon ground ginger
6 cups chicken stock
salt and pepper to taste

#3 Ingredients
1 teaspoon ground cumin
1 tablespoon Worcestershire sauce

Topper/diced green onions

- Brown and drain the #1 ingredients and combine all the #1 and #2 ingredients in a large soup pot. Bring to a simmer for 45 minutes. Add the #3 ingredients and continue to simmer for another 15 minutes. Serve.

Goes well with *Mustard, Cheese, and Onion Popovers*, page 197.

A Gumbo from the Bayou

about 7 16-ounce servings

#1 Ingredient
1 cup mild sausage, sliced

#2 Ingredients
1 cup chicken, cut into bite-sized pieces
1 pound shrimp, peeled and deveined
1/2 cup onion, chopped
1/2 cup green bell pepper, chopped
1 teaspoon garlic, minced
2 cups fresh okra, sliced, or 1 10-ounce package frozen sliced or cut okra, defrosted

1/2 teaspoon ground cayenne pepper or to taste
2 14-ounce can stewed tomatoes
1 teaspoon Old Bay seasoning
6 cups chicken stock
salt to taste

#3 Ingredient
1/2 cup uncooked minute rice

Topper/sour cream with a sprinkle of Old Bay seasoning

- Brown and drain the #1 ingredient and combine the #1 and #2 ingredients in a large soup pot and bring to a simmer for 20 minutes. Add the #3 ingredient and let sit 5 minutes.

Goes well with *Tiny Shrimp Biscuits*, page 172.

Mancha Manteles

SPICY CHICKEN STEW WITH FRUIT,
A GOOD WAY TO ESCAPE THE DOLDRUMS

about 6 16-ounce servings

#1 Ingredients
1 cup boneless chicken, cut into
bite-sized pieces
1 cup pork stew meat, finely diced
1 cup onion, diced small
1/2 cup bell pepper, chopped
small
1 14-ounce can tomato sauce
1 tablespoon chili powder
2 teaspoons cinnamon
1 cup sweet potatoes, peeled and
diced small

2 tablespoons fresh parsley, chopped
6 cups chicken stock
salt to taste

#2 Ingredient
2 cups Granny Smith apples,
peeled and diced small

#3 Ingredient
3 bananas, sliced

Topper/you pick one!

- Combine the #1 ingredients in a large soup pot and bring to a simmer for 45 minutes or until the pork is tender.
- Add the #2 ingredient and continue to simmer for another 20 minutes. Add the #3 ingredient and stir. Let heat through and serve.

* get ready for a delicious surprise *

Goes well with *Apple Fritters*, page 204.

Egg Drop Soup

about 3 16-ounce servings

#1 Ingredients
1/3 cup fresh parsley, minced
1/2 cup leeks (whites only), sliced
thin
1/2 cup fresh sweet peas with
shells, or 1/2 cup frozen peas
6 cups chicken stock
salt and white pepper to taste

#2 Ingredient
2 eggs, well beaten

Topper/sliced green onions

- Combine all the #1 ingredients in a large soup pot and bring to a simmer for 15 minutes. Slowly drizzle the #2 ingredient into the #1 ingredients and let simmer another 15 minutes. Serve.

Goes well with *Tsung Yu Ping Flat Bread Chinese Onion Circles*, page 208.

Chapter 6

SOUPS MADE WITH PORK AND PORK PRODUCTS

Also see *Chapter 2* for bean soups that include bacon, ham and sausage.

Tomato Rice Soup

SIMPLE AND GOOD!

about 5 16-ounce servings

#1 Ingredients
6 slices bacon, diced
1/2 cup onion, diced small
1/2 pound mild sausage

#2 Ingredients
4 cups chicken stock
2 14-ounce cans stewed tomatoes
salt and pepper to taste

#3 Ingredient
1/2 cup uncooked minute rice

Topper/toasted sesame seeds

• Brown the #1 ingredients and drain.
• Combine the #1 and #2 ingredients in a large soup pot and bring to a simmer for 20 minutes. Add the #3 ingredient, wait 5 minutes, and serve.

Goes well with *Sun-Dried Tomato and Cheese Biscuits*, page 179.

Pasta and Salami With Green Olives

about 4 16-ounce servings

#1 Ingredients
6 cups chicken stock
2 cups your favorite salami, diced
1/2 cup onion, diced
1/2 cup red bell pepper, diced
salt and pepper to taste

#2 Ingredient
1 cup large elbow macaroni, uncooked

Topper/Parmesan cheese with diced raw onions

• Combine the #1 ingredients in a large soup pot and bring to a simmer for 30 minutes. Add the #2 ingredient and continue to simmer for another 10 minutes, or until the pasta is tender. Serve.

Goes well with *Italian Sesame Seed Bread Sticks*, page 199.

Veggie and Canadian Bacon Chowder

about 7 16-ounce servings

#1 Ingredients
6 cups chicken stock
2 cups Canadian bacon, diced
   small
1/2 cup carrots, grated
1 cup celery, diced small
1 15-ounce can French-styled
   green beans, drained
1 cup packed cabbage, chopped
salt and pepper to taste

#2 Ingredients
1 cup half-and-half
1 cup sour cream

Topper/sliced black olives

- Mix the #2 ingredients together with a fork and set aside.
- Combine the #1 ingredients in a large soup pot and bring to a simmer for 30 minutes. Slowly add the #2 ingredients, stirring constantly until reheated, and serve.

Goes well with *French Fried Onion Biscuits*, page 169.

French Peasant Soup

about 6 16-ounce servings

#1 Ingredients
4 slices bacon, diced
1 cup mild sausage, ground
1 cup onion, chopped

#2 Ingredients
6 cups chicken stock
1 15-ounce can navy beans,
   rinsed and drained
2 cups packed cabbage,
   chopped

1 medium turnip, peeled and
   diced
1/2 cup carrots, sliced thin
1 cup leeks, sliced (whites only)
1 teaspoon garlic, minced, or
   1/2 teaspoon garlic powder
1/2 tablespoon fresh thyme,
   chopped
salt and pepper to taste

Topper/canned French fried onions

- Brown and drain the #1 ingredients. Combine the #1 and #2 ingredients together in a large soup pot and bring to a simmer for 45 minutes. Serve.

Goes well with *Bacon and Cheese Biscuits*, page 172.

Italian Sausage with White Beans

about 6 16-ounce servings

#1 Ingredient
2 cups mild Italian sausage, ground

#2 Ingredients
6 cups chicken stock
1 15-ounce can navy beans, with
  liquid
1 teaspoon garlic, minced, or 1/2
  teaspoon garlic powder
1 cup onion, chopped
1/2 cup carrots, grated

1 cup celery, diced small
2 cups chicken stock
2 14-ounce cans stewed tomatoes
salt and pepper to taste

#3 Ingredient
1 cup large elbow macaroni,
  uncooked

Topper/mozzarella cheese,
  shredded

- Brown and drain the #1 ingredient.
- Combine with the #2 ingredients in a large soup pot and bring to a simmer for 45 minutes. Add the #3 ingredients, continue to simmer for another 15 minutes, and serve.

Goes well with *Italian Sesame Seed Bread Sticks*, page 199.

Italian Zuppa Alla Menta

ITALIAN MINT SOUP

about 6 16-ounce servings

#1 Ingredients
8 slices of bacon, diced
1 cup onion, diced small

#2 Ingredients
6 cups chicken stock
2 cups tomato, diced

1 cup zucchini, diced
2 potatoes, peeled and diced
3/4 cup fresh mint, chopped
salt and pepper to taste

Topper/fresh mint leaves

- Brown and drain the #1 ingredients. Combine with the #1 and #2 ingredients in a large soup pot and bring to a simmer for 45 minutes, or until the veggies are tender. Serve.

Goes well with *Herb and Onion Loaf*, page 131.

Potato Pepperoni Soup

about 6 16-ounce servings

#1 Ingredient
1 cup pepperoni, diced small

½ cup onions, diced small
salt and pepper to taste

#2 Ingredients
4 cups chicken stock
4 cups potatoes, peeled and diced
½ cup celery, diced small
½ cup carrots, grated

#3 Ingredients
1 cup half-and-half
1 cup sour cream

Topper/mozzarella cheese, grated

- Mix the #3 ingredients with a wire whisk and set aside.
- Sauté the #1 ingredient and drain. Combine the #1 and #2 ingredients in a large soup pot and bring to a simmer for 45 minutes. Slowly add the #3 ingredients, stirring constantly until reheated. Serve.

Goes well with *Tall Biscuits*, page 168.

Mock Turtle Soup

about 6 16-ounce servings

#1 Ingredients
4 cups beef stock
2 cups pork meat, cut into bite-
  sized pieces
1 cup onion, chopped
½ cup celery, diced small
½ cup green bell pepper, diced
  small
2 14-ounce cans stewed tomatoes
½ tablespoon fresh thyme,
  chopped

¼ teaspoon ground allspice
1 small bay leaf
salt and pepper to taste

#2 Ingredient
1 cup sherry

#3 Ingredient
4 hard-boiled eggs, chopped

Topper/thinly sliced lemons

- Boil the #3 ingredient, then cool, peel, chop, and set aside.
- Combine the #1 ingredients in a large soup pot and bring to a simmer for 45 minutes. Add the #2 ingredient and continue to simmer for 5 minutes. Add the #3 ingredient and continue to simmer another 5 minutes. Serve.

Goes well with *Pecan Popovers*, page 197.

German Knockwurst Chowder

about 5 16-ounce servings

#1 Ingredients
4 cups chicken stock
2 cups knockwurst, cut into bite-sized pieces
1/2 cup celery, diced small
1/2 cup carrots, grated
1 cup packed cabbage, shredded
1 tablespoon caraway seeds
salt and white pepper to taste

#2 Ingredients
1 cup half-and-half
1 cup sour cream

Topper/sour cream mixed with a touch of Dijon mustard and chives

• Mix the #2 ingredients with a wire whisk and set aside. Combine all the #1 ingredients in a large soup pot and bring to a simmer for 30 minutes. Slowly add the #2 ingredients, stirring constantly until reheated, and serve.

Goes well with *Quick Onion Rye with Caraway Seeds*, page 159.

Ecuador's Pork and Beer Stew

about 6 16-ounce servings

#1 Ingredients
3 12-ounce cans of your favorite beer
2 cups pork, cut into bite-sized pieces
1 teaspoon garlic, minced
1 cup onion, chopped
2 14-ounce cans stewed tomatoes
1 very small Serrano (red) chile, finely chopped with seeds removed
3 tablespoons fresh cilantro, chopped
1 teaspoon ground cumin
1 teaspoon fresh oregano, chopped, or 1/2 teaspoon dry oregano flakes
salt and pepper to taste

#2 Ingredient
1/2 cup uncooked minute rice

Topper/diced red and green onion

• Combine the #1 ingredients in a large soup pot and bring to a simmer for 40 minutes, or until the meat is tender. Add the #2 ingredient, wait 5 minutes, and serve.

Goes well with *Corn Bread*, page 183.

Old Southern-Style Ham and Shrimp Gumbo

about 8 16-ounce servings

#1 Ingredients
6 cups chicken stock
2 cups smoked ham, cut into bite-sized pieces
1/2 cup carrots, diced small
1/2 cup red bell pepper, chopped
1/2 cup onion, chopped
2 cups fresh okra, sliced, or 1 10-ounce package frozen sliced or cut okra, defrosted
2 14-ounce cans stewed tomatoes
tabasco to taste
salt and white pepper to taste

#2 Ingredient
2 cups shrimp, de-veined and peeled

#3 Ingredient
1/2 cup uncooked minute rice

Topper/shredded cheddar with diced onion

- Combine the #1 ingredients together in a large soup pot and bring to a simmer for 30 minutes. Add the #2 ingredient and continue to simmer for 5 minutes. Add the #3 ingredient, let sit for 5 minutes, and serve.

Goes well with *your choice of quickbread.*

Kielbasa Stew

ONE OF MY FAVORITES

about 8 16-ounce servings

#1 Ingredients
4 cups chicken stock
4 cups kielbasa sausage, cut into bite-sized pieces
2 14-ounce cans stewed tomatoes
1/2 cup carrots, grated
1 15-ounce can kidney beans, with liquid
1/2 cup bell pepper, diced small
1 cup onion, diced small
2 cups cabbage, chopped and packed
salt and pepper to taste

#2 Ingredient
1/2 cup minute rice

Topper/ripe avocado, diced

- Combine the #1 ingredients, and bring to a simmer for 45 minutes. Add the #2 ingredient, let sit 5 minutes, and serve.

Goes well with *Buttery Beer Bread, page 133.*

Posole

about 7 16-ounce servings

#1 Ingredients
6 cups chicken stock
2 cups pork meat, cut into bite-
  sized pieces
1/2 cup carrots, sliced thin
1 cup onion, chopped
1 cup celery, sliced
1 teaspoon garlic, minced, or 1/2
  teaspoon garlic powder
1 15-ounce can pinto beans, drained
1 15-ounce can yellow hominy,
  drained

1 teaspoon chili powder or to
  taste
1 teaspoon dried oregano
3 tablespoon fresh cilantro,
  chopped
salt and pepper to taste

#2 Ingredient
bag of your favorite tortilla
  chips

Topper/thinly sliced limes

• Combine the #1 ingredients in a large soup pot and bring to a simmer for
  45 minutes. Place a portion of tortilla chips in each bowl, pour the soup
  over them, and serve.

Goes well with *Salsa Loaf*, page 140.

Spanish Valencia Soup

about 6 16-ounce servings

#1 Ingredients
2 cups ham, cut into bite-sized pieces
2 cups packed cabbage, chopped
1 cup onion, diced small
1/4 cup fresh cilantro, chopped
1/4 cup fresh parsley, chopped
2 14-ounce cans diced tomatoes
1/2 teaspoon chili powder

1 teaspoon ground cumin
4 cups chicken stock
salt and pepper to taste

#2 Ingredient
1/2 cup minute rice

Topper/tortilla chips

• Combine all the #1 ingredients in a large soup pot and bring to a simmer
  for 45 minutes, or until the veggies are tender. Add the #2 ingredient, wait
  5 minutes, and serve.

Goes well with *Frito Corn Bread*, page 187.

Ma Po Tofu Soup

THIS CAN BE VERY SPICY, SO WATCH OUT!

about 5 16-ounce servings

#1 Ingredients
1 tablespoon fermented black
    beans
2 cups ground pork

#2 Ingredients
6 cups chicken stock
1 tablespoon fresh ginger
    minced
1 tablespoon garlic, minced

1 small dried red chili, minced, or
    to taste
4 peppercorns, crushed
1/4 teaspoon hot bean paste or to
    taste
ground cayenne pepper to taste
1 10-ounce block firm tofu, diced
salt to taste

Topper/you pick one!

• Brown and drain the #1 ingredients. Combine the #1 and #2 ingredients in
  a large soup pot and bring to a simmer for 30 minutes. Serve.

Goes well with *Sesame Seed Crackers*, page 201.

Chapter 7

SOUPS MADE WITH BEEF

You can also use venison, elk, buffalo, or moose. With wild game, your cooking times are basically the same, but it is a good idea to brown the meats first. Also, if you want to get rid of that gamy taste, it is recommended that you soak the meat for 30 minutes in salted water or milk before cooking. Another tip is to remove all the fat before cooking. The herb sage is also good for hiding that game taste.

Steak and Mushroom Soup

FINALLY SOMETHING TO DO WITH LEFTOVER STEAK,
IT'S EVEN BETTER AFTER BEING BARBEQUED.

about 5 16-ounce servings

#1 Ingredients
4 cups beef stock
2 cups leftover steak, sliced
1 cup fresh mushrooms,
    sliced
1 cup onion, chopped
1/2 teaspoon garlic, minced
1 tablespoon your favorite
    barbeque sauce

1 cup zucchini, sliced
1 tablespoon Dijon mustard
salt and pepper to taste

#2 Ingredient
2 cups beer

Topper/sour cream mixed with
    horseradish (to taste)

- Combine the #1 ingredients in a large soup pot and bring to a simmer for 20 minutes. Add the #2 ingredient and continue to simmer for another 5 minutes. Serve.

Goes well with *Sun-Dried Tomato and Onion Buttermilk Biscuits*, page 179.

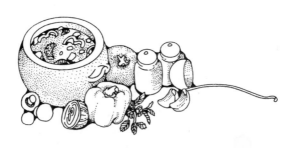

Beef Barley Soup

about 7 16-ounce servings

#1 Ingredients

6 cups beef stock
2 cups stew meat, cut into bite-
    sized pieces
1 cup celery, sliced
1 cup onion, diced
1 cup carrots, sliced
2 cups fresh mushrooms, sliced

1 cup quick-cooking barley
1 teaspoon fresh dill weed
1 teaspoon garlic, minced
1 small dried bay leaf
salt and pepper to taste

Topper/sour cream with
    horseradish mixed in (to taste)

• Combine the #1 ingredients in a large soup pot and bring to a simmer of 45 minutes, or until the meat is tender. Serve.

Goes well with *Poppy Seed and Buttermilk Biscuits,*, page 174.

Pezzaniti's Minestrone

about 7 16-ounce servings

#1 Ingredients

1 pound ground beef
1/2 pound Italian sausage, ground

#2 Ingredients

4 cups beef stock
1 cup onion, chopped
1/2 cup carrots, thinly sliced
1/2 cup celery, thinly sliced
2 14-ounce cans Italian stewed
    tomatoes
1 small dried bay leaf
1 teaspoon each: fresh thyme,
    basil, and oregano, minced

1 teaspoon garlic, minced
1 15-ounce can kidney beans,
    drained
1 cup zucchini, diced
1 cup cabbage, chopped and
    packed
salt and pepper to taste

#3 Ingredient

1 cup uncooked large elbow, shell,
    or any other large macaroni

Topper/Parmesan cheese

• Cook, rinse, and drain the #3 ingredients. Set aside.
• Brown the #1 ingredients and drain. Combine the #1 and #2 ingredients in a large soup pot, and bring to a simmer for 45 minutes, or until the veggies are tender. Add the #3 ingredient, give a good stir, and serve.

Goes well with *Italian Sesame Seed Bread Sticks*, page 199.

Tomato and Sauerkraut Soup

IT'S GOOD, REALLY!

about 7 16-ounce servings

#1 Ingredients
6 cups beef stock
2 cups stew beef, cut into bite-
   sized pieces
1 14-ounce can sauerkraut with
   liquid
2 14-ounce cans stewed tomatoes
salt and pepper to taste

#2 Ingredients
2½ teaspoons sugar
3 tablespoons lemon juice

Topper/grated carrot

- Mix the #2 ingredients and set aside.
- Combine the #1 ingredients in a large soup pot and bring to a simmer for 45 minutes, or until the meat is tender. Add the #2 ingredients and continue to simmer another 5 minutes. Serve.

Goes well with *Celery-Poppy Seed-Onion Bread*, page 129.

Jardiniere Soup

about 8 16-ounce servings

#1 Ingredients
6 cups beef stock
2 cups stew beef, cut into bite-
   sized pieces
1 cup onion, chopped
2 cups potatoes, peeled and diced
   into bite-sized pieces
1 cup fresh, shelled sweet peas, or
   1 cup, frozen
1 cup fresh green beans, cut, or 1
   cup, frozen and cut
2 14-ounce cans stewed tomatoes
salt and pepper to taste

#2 Ingredient
2 cups cabbage, shredded and packed

Topper/garlic croutons

- Combine the #1 ingredients in a large soup pot and bring to a simmer for 45 minutes, or until the meat is tender. Add the #2 ingredient and continue to simmer for another 15 to 20 minutes. Serve.

Goes well with *Basic Bread Sticks,* page 198.

Stifado

A GREEK SOUP

about 6 16-ounce servings

#1 Ingredients
1 cup onion, chopped
2 teaspoons garlic, minced
1 tablespoon olive oil
2 cups beef stew meat, cut into
   bite-sized pieces

#2 Ingredients
6 cups beef stock
2 tablespoons red wine vinegar
1/2 teaspoon ground pepper
1 small dried bay leaf
1 cinnamon stick
1 14-ounce can stewed tomatoes
1 cup pearl onions, peeled
salt and pepper to taste

Topper/crumbled Feta cheese

• Brown and drain the #1 ingredients. Combine the #1 and #2 ingredients in a large soup pot, and bring to a simmer for 30 minutes, or until the meat is tender. Serve.

Goes well with *French Fried Onion Biscuits*, page 169.

Taco Soup

THANKS, VIOLA!

about 5 16-ounce servings

#1 Ingredient
1 pound hamburger

#2 Ingredient
2 1-ounce envelopes of taco
seasoning mix

#3 Ingredients
4 cups beef stock
1 cup frozen corn
2 14-ounce cans stewed tomatoes
1 cup onion, finely chopped
salt and pepper to taste

Topper/bunch of corn chips

• Brown and drain the #1 ingredient.
• Combine the #1 and #2 ingredients in a large soup pot. Do not follow the package directions on seasoning. Add the #3 ingredients, bring to a simmer for 30 minutes, and serve.

Goes well with *Mexican Corn Bread*, page 188.

Peccadillo Soup From Mexico

about 6 16-ounce servings

#1 Ingredient
1 pound hamburger

#2 Ingredients
4 cups beef stock
1 cup onion, diced small
1/2 tablespoon garlic, minced
1 14-ounce can stewed tomatoes
1 15-ounce can kidney beans,
    drained
1/2 tablespoon chili powder

1 teaspoon ground cumin
2 tablespoon sugar
1 6-ounce can black olives, pitted
    and chopped
salt and pepper to taste

#3 Ingredient
1/2 cup uncooked minute rice

Topper/grated Romano cheese

- Brown and drain the #1 ingredient.
- Combine the #1 and #2 ingredients in a large soup pot and bring to a simmer for 30 minutes. Add the #3 ingredients, let set for 5 minutes, and serve.

Goes well with *Cheesy Cream-Style Corn Bread*, page 185.

Mexican Noodle Soup

about 6 16-ounce servings

#1 Ingredient
1 pound hamburger

#2 Ingredients
4 cups beef stock
1/2 cup celery, thinly sliced
1/2 cup green olives, with pimento,
    chopped (salad olives)
2 14-ounce cans stewed
    tomatoes
1 tablespoon chili powder
1 teaspoon garlic, minced

1 cup fresh corn, cut off the cob,
    or 1 cup, frozen
1 teaspoon ground cumin
1 teaspoon fresh oregano, minced
salt and pepper to taste

#3 Ingredient
1 cup large elbow macaroni,
    uncooked

Topper/grated cheese of your
    choice

- Brown and drain the #1 ingredient.
- Combine the #1 and #2 ingredients in a soup pot and bring to a simmer for 45 minutes, or until the veggies are tender. Add the #3 ingredients, continue to simmer for another 10 minutes, and serve.

Goes well with *Frito Corn Bread*, page 187.

Easy Albondiagas Mexican Meat Soup

about 6 16-ounce servings

#1 Ingredients
1/2 pound hamburger
1/2 pound pork sausage

#2 Ingredients
4 cups beef stock
1 teaspoon chili powder
2 tablespoons dried onion flakes
4 14-ounce cans stewed
   tomatoes

1 cup fresh corn, cut off the cob,
   or 1 cup, frozen
1 15-ounce can chili beans
salt and pepper to taste

#3 Ingredient
1/2 cup uncooked minute rice

Topper/sour cream with diced
   red onion

- Brown and drain the #1 ingredients.
- Combine the #1 and #2 ingredient in a large soup pot and bring to a simmer for 45 minutes. Add the #3 ingredient, wait 5 minutes, and serve.

Goes well with *Cheese Popovers*, page 197.

Hot Salsa Chili

about 7 16-ounce servings

#1 Ingredients
1/2 pound spicy Italian sausage,
   ground
1/2 pound hamburger

#2 Ingredients
2 cups beef stock
4 cups hot salsa
1 cup onion, chopped
2 large tomatoes, chopped
2 tablespoons chili powder
2 teaspoons hot Hungarian paprika

1 tablespoon fresh oregano,
   minced
1 1/2 teaspoon cumin, ground
4 teaspoons liquid cayenne pepper
minced jalapeño chilies to taste
1/2 cup bell pepper, chopped
4 tablespoons fresh cilantro,
   chopped
1 15-ounce kidney beans, drained
salt to taste

Topper/grated jalapeño cheese

- Brown and drain the #1 ingredients.
- Combine the #1 and #2 ingredients in a large soup pot and bring to a simmer for 30 minutes. Serve.

Goes well with *Mexican Corn Bread*, page 188.

Hot New Orleans Chili

about 7 16-ounce servings

#1 Ingredient
1 pound hamburger

#2 Ingredients
6 cups beef stock
1 cup onion, chopped
1/2 cup green bell pepper, chopped
1/2 cup red bell pepper, chopped
1/2 tablespoon fresh garlic, minced
2 14-ounce cans stewed tomatoes
1 15-ounce can black-eyed peas,
  with liquid
2 cups fresh spinach, chopped, or
  1 10-ounce package frozen
  spinach, defrosted, with liquid
  squeezed out

1 cup fresh corn, cut from the
  cob, or 1 cup, frozen
2 tablespoons chili powder or to
  taste
1 teaspoon ground cayenne
  pepper or to taste
1 teaspoon ground cumin
salt and pepper to taste

#3 Ingredient
1/2 cup uncooked minute rice

Topper/lemon juice and fresh
chives

- Brown and drain the #1 ingredient.
- Combine the #1 and #2 ingredients in a large soup pot and bring to a simmer
  for 45 minutes. Add the #2 ingredient, wait 5 minutes, and serve.

Goes well with *Simple Biscuits*, page 167.

Empty-the-Fridge-of-Leftovers Soup

about 5 16-ounce servings

#1 Ingredients
6 cups beef stock
2 cups cooked meat, diced or
  ground
1 cup of any kind of vegetable
1 cup onion, chopped
1 cup uncooked pasta, or
  potatoes, peeled and diced
anything else that smells okay

#2 Ingredient
1/2 cup of minute rice (if not using
  pasta or potatoes)

Topper/your choice

- Combine the #1 ingredients in a large soup pot and bring to a simmer until
  the ingredients that are raw are cooked, usually 20 minutes. If you use the
  #2 ingredient add, wait 5 minutes, and serve.

Goes well with *Buttery Beer Bread*, page 133.

Venison Chili

REMEMBER YOU CAN USE OTHER MEATS. SEE TOP OF PAGE 65.

about 7 16-ounce servings

#1 Ingredients
4 cups beef stock
2 cups venison stew meat, cut into
  bite-sized pieces
2 14-ounce cans stewed tomatoes
1/2 cup green bell pepper, chopped
1 15-ounce can kidney beans,
  with liquid
1 tablespoon chili powder
2 teaspoons cayenne pepper,
  ground
2 teaspoons cumin, ground

1 teaspoon fresh oregano, minced
1 cup onion, chopped
2 teaspoons garlic, minced
2 1/2 tablespoons barbeque sauce
1 12-ounce can of your favorite
  beer
1 3-ounce can chopped jalapeño
  peppers (optional)
salt and pepper to taste

Topper/crushed corn chips and
  diced onion

- Combine the #1 ingredients in a large soup pot and bring to a simmer for 45 minutes, or until the venison is tender. Serve

Goes well with *Buttery Beer Bread*, page 133.

Sharon's Quick Beef Stew

about 7 16-ounce servings

#1 Ingredients
1 pound hamburger
1 cup onion, chopped

#2 Ingredients
6 cups beef stock
1 14-ounce can stewed tomatoes
1/2 teaspoon fresh basil, chopped

1/2 16-ounce package frozen
  mixed vegetables, (broccoli,
  carrots and cauliflower)
salt and pepper to taste

Topper/horseradish and sour
  cream, mixed to taste

- Brown and drain the #1 ingredients.
- Combine the #1 and #2 ingredients in a large soup pot and bring to a simmer for 30 minutes. Serve.

Goes well with *Easy Popovers*, page 196.

'Been-Working-Cattle-All-Day-and-They're-Coming-in-Hungry' Stew

about 15 16-ounce servings

#1 Ingredient
1 pound hamburger

#2 Ingredients
10 cups beef stock
3 cups stew beef, cut into bite-sized pieces
6 large potatoes, peeled and diced
6 small carrots, sliced 1/4 inch thick
4 medium stalks celery, sliced 1/4 inch thick
2 large onions, chopped
1 cup fresh corn, cut off the cob, or 1 cup, frozen

4 large tomatoes, diced
1 cup bell pepper, chopped
2 teaspoons dry onion flakes
3 12-ounce cans of beer
1 cup frozen baby lima beans
1 cup fresh spinach, chopped and packed
add water if needed

#3 Ingredient
4 1-ounce envelopes brown gravy mix, prepared according to package directions

Topper/horseradish (to taste)

- Brown the #1 ingredient, drain.
- Combine the #1 ingredient with the #2 ingredients in a 12-quart soup pot and simmer for 1 hour or until the veggies and beef are tender. Just before serving, pre-mix the #3 ingredients, using juice from the soup (usually 4 cups). Add this mixture to the stew, give a good stir, and serve.

Goes well with *Onion and Parmesan Buttermilk Biscuits*, page 178.

My friend Linda from Cody, Wyoming, and I have been known to feed 10 very hungry men with this recipe, with enough for seconds. A huge tossed salad, a mountain of biscuits, and lots of pie and coffee for desert, this always puts them to sleep for at least an hour. The men are then ready to go back to work.

Meatball Stew

about 6 16-ounce servings

#1 Ingredients
1 pound hamburger
1 1-ounce envelope spaghetti
sauce mix
1 cup Italian bread crumbs
1 egg

#2 Ingredients
4 cups beef stock
1 cup onion, chopped
6 tablespoons fresh parsley,
chopped

2 14-ounce cans stewed tomatoes
1/2 cup carrots, thinly sliced
2 medium sized potatoes, peeled
and diced
1/2 cup celery, thinly sliced
2 tablespoons fresh basil, minced
1 tablespoon fresh oregano,
minced
1 small dried bay leaf
salt and pepper to taste

Topper/grated Parmesan cheese

• Mix the #1 ingredients together and make bite-sized meat balls. Bake at 450° for 15 or 20 minutes, or until the meat balls are done. Drain. Combine the #2 ingredients in a large soup pot and simmer for 30 minutes, or until the veggies are tender. Add the #1 ingredients, reheat, and serve.

Goes well with *Celery-Poppy Seed-Onion Bread*, page 129.

African Beef and Vegetable Stew

about 6 16-ounce servings

#1 Ingredients
6 cups beef stock
2 cups stew beef, cut into bite-
sized pieces
2 cups Hubbards squash, peeled,
and diced small
1/4 teaspoon ground ginger or to
taste

1/4 teaspoon ground cayenne
pepper or to taste
2 large tomatoes, chopped
1 10-ounce package frozen baby
lima beans

Topper/diced raw onions

• Combine the #1 ingredients and bring to a simmer for 1 hour or until the meat is tender.

Goes well with *Herb and Onion Loaf*, page 131.

Italian Beef Stew

about 7 16-ounce servings

#1 Ingredients
4 cups beef stock
2 cups stew beef, cut into bite-
  sized pieces
1/2 cup onion, chopped
1/2 cup celery, sliced
1/2 cup carrots, sliced
1 cup zucchini, sliced
1/2 cup frozen corn
1/2 cup bell pepper, chopped
1 15-ounce can kidney beans,
  with liquid

2 14-ounce cans Italian stewed
  tomatoes
1/2 tablespoon garlic, minced, or
  to taste
1 1/2 teaspoons fresh oregano,
  minced
1 1/2 teaspoons fresh basil, minced
1/2 teaspoon onion powder
salt and pepper to taste

Topper/sour cream with fresh
chives, sliced

• Combine the #1 ingredients together in a large soup pot and bring to a simmer for 45 minutes, or until the meat is tender. Serve.

Goes well with *your choice of quickbread.*

Asian Beef Stew

THE QUICK VERSION

about 8 16-ounce servings

#1 Ingredients
5 cups beef stock
2 cups stew beef, cut into bite-
  sized pieces
1 15-ounce can kidney beans,
  with the liquid
1 cup onion, diced small
1 14-ounce can stewed tomatoes
1/2 teaspoon ground cayenne
  pepper or to taste
salt to taste

#2 Ingredients
2 cups milk
1 16-ounce can of split pea soup
1 tablespoon fresh dill weed, or
  1/2 tablespoon, dried

Topper/sliced hard-boiled eggs

• Mix the #2 ingredients together with a wire whisk and set aside.
• Combine the #1 ingredients in a large soup pot and bring to a simmer for 45 minutes. Slowly add the #2 ingredients, stirring constantly until reheated, and serve.

Goes well with *Poppy Seed Cheese and Chive Bread*, page 139.

Quick and Easy Beef Stew with Dumplings

about 6 16-ounce servings

#1 Ingredients
6 cups beef stock
1 cup stew meat, cut into bite-
  sized pieces
1 1-ounce envelope onion soup mix
1 cup onion, diced small
1 cup celery, thinly sliced
1/2 cup carrots, grated
2 cups mushrooms, sliced

2 tablespoons fresh marjoram,
  minced or 1 tablespoon, dried
1 teaspoon garlic, minced
2 14-ounce cans stewed tomatoes
1 tablespoon fresh parsley,
  chopped
salt and pepper to taste

Topper/the dumplings

- Combine the #1 ingredients together in a large soup pot and bring to a simmer for 30 minutes.
- Follow the recipe for *Basic Drop Biscuits*, page 181, but don't bake them. Drop by the tablespoon, a heaping amount of dough at a time, gently pushing the dumpling down in the soup. Wait 5 seconds and let it float to the top.
- Repeat with the rest of the dough. Bring to a simmer, cover, and continue to simmer for 20 minutes. Serve.

Tequila Stew

about 5 16-ounce servings

#1 Ingredients
6 slices bacon, diced
2 cups stew beef, cut into
  bite-sized pieces

#2 Ingredients
6 cups beef stock
1 cup onion, chopped
1/2 cup celery, sliced
1 15-ounce can garbanzo beans,
  drained

1 teaspoon garlic, minced
1 tablespoon fresh cilantro, chopped
salt and pepper to taste

#3 Ingredient
2/3 cup tequila

Topper/you pick one!

- Brown and drain the #1 ingredients. Combine the #1 and #2 ingredients in a large soup pot, and bring to a simmer for 20 minutes. Add the #3 ingredients, continue to simmer for another 10 minutes. Serve.

Goes well with *Veggie Bread*, page 128.

Chapter 8

SOUPS MADE WITH LAMB

Winter Barley Soup
about 6 16-ounce servings

#1 Ingredients

6 cups chicken stock
2 cups lamb meat, cut into bite-
   sized pieces
1 cup onion, chopped
1 cup celery, sliced
1 cup carrots, sliced
1/2 cup green bell pepper,
   chopped

1/4 cup fresh parsley, chopped, or
   2 tablespoons, dried
1/2 tablespoon fresh thyme,
   minced, or 1/4 tablespoon, dried
1 dried bay leaf
1/2 cup long cooking barley
salt and pepper to taste

Topper/diced tomatoes and
   onions

• Combine the #1 ingredients in a large soup pot and bring to a simmer for
   45 minutes. Serve.

Goes well with *Celery and Onion Buttermilk Bread*, page 136.

Lamb Stew
about 6 16-ounce servings

#1 Ingredients

6 cups beef stock
2 cups lamb stew meat, cut into
   bite-sized pieces
3 teaspoons fresh oregano, or 1
   teaspoon, dried
1 cup onion, chopped
1 teaspoon garlic, minced, or 1/2
   teaspoon garlic powder

1 cup potato, peeled and diced
1 cup celery, sliced
1 cup carrots, sliced
salt and white pepper to taste

Topper/sour cream with crushed
   mint leaves

• Combine the #1 ingredients in a large soup pot and bring to a simmer for
   45 minutes, or until the meat is tender. Serve.

Goes well with *Fresh Apple Bread*, page 148.

Irish Stew

about 6 16-ounce servings

#1 Ingredients
6 cups beef stock
2 cups lamb stew meat, diced
    small
2 cups potatoes, peeled and diced
    into bite-sized pieces
1 cup onion, chopped
1 cup carrots, sliced

1 cup turnip, peeled and diced
    small
2 tablespoons fresh parsley,
    chopped, or 3 tablespoons,
    dried
salt and pepper to taste

Topper/sliced hard-boiled egg

• Combine the #1 ingredients together in a large soup pot and bring to a simmer for 45 minutes. Serve.

Goes well with *Casserole Millet Bread with Herbs*, page 159.

Curried Lamb Stew

about 7 16-ounce servings

#1 Ingredients
6 cups beef stock
2 cups lamb stew meat, cut into
    bite-sized pieces
1 cup onion, chopped
1 teaspoon garlic, minced, or 1/2
    teaspoon garlic powder
1 cup potatoes, peeled and diced
1/2 cup celery, sliced
1/2 tablespoon curry powder
1/2 teaspoon ground turmeric

1/2 teaspoon ground cumin
1 large Granny Smith apple,
    peeled and diced
salt and white pepper to taste

#2 Ingredients
1 cup sour cream
1 cup milk

Topper/roasted peanuts and
    toasted coconut

• Mix the #2 ingredients together with a wire whisk and set aside.
• Combine the #1 ingredients in a large soup pot and bring to a simmer for 45 minutes, or until the meat is tender. Slowly add the #2 ingredients, stirring constantly until reheated, and serve.

Goes well with *Mustardy Cheese Bread*, page 142.

Lamb Stew with Mustard

about 6 16-ounce servings

#1 Ingredients
2 cups lamb meat, cut into bite-
    sized pieces
1/2 cup onion, chopped

1/2 cup carrots, grated
1 cup celery, diced
1 cup frozen corn
salt and pepper to taste

#2 Ingredients
4 cups chicken stock
2 14-ounce cans stewed
    tomatoes
1 teaspoon fresh rosemary, or 1/2
    teaspoon, dried

#3 Ingredients
1 pint half-and-half
2 tablespoons of your favorite
    mustard

Topper/you pick one!

- Mix the #3 ingredients together with a wire whisk set aside.
- Brown and drain the #1 ingredients. Add to the #2 ingredients in a large soup pot, and bring to a simmer for 45 minutes, or until the meat is tender. Slowly add the #3 ingredients stirring constantly until reheated, and serve.

Goes well with *Mustardy Cheese Bread*, page 142.

Lamb Ragout

about 6 16-ounce servings

#1 Ingredients
6 cups chicken stock
2 cups lamb meat, cut into bite-
    sized pieces
1 teaspoon garlic, minced, or 1/2
    teaspoon garlic powder
1 cup onion, chopped
1 dried bay leaf
1 tablespoon fresh mint leaves,
    chopped, or 1/2 tablespoon,
    dried

1 teaspoon fresh rosemary,
    minced, or 1/2 teaspoon, dried
2 cups potatoes, peeled and diced
1/2 cup carrots, chopped
1 teaspoon dried celery seed
salt and white pepper to taste

Topper/mint jelly

- Combine the #1 ingredients in a large soup pot and bring to a simmer for 45 minutes. Serve.

Goes well with *Whole Wheat and Wheat Germ Crackers*, page 201.

Chapter 9

SOUPS MADE WITH SEAFOOD

Manhattan Clam Chowder

about 6 16-ounce servings

#1 Ingredients
2 cups fish or chicken stock
2 6-ounce cans minced clams,
  with the liquid
2 6-ounce cans chopped clams,
  with the liquid
1 6-ounce can baby clams, with
  the liquid
1/2 cup onion, diced very small
1/2 cup carrots, grated

2 cups potatoes, peeled and diced
  very small
2 8-ounce bottles clam juice
2 14-ounce can Italian stewed
  tomatoes
1/4 teaspoon dried thyme
salt and pepper to taste

Topper/shredded Colby cheese

• Combine the ingredients in a large soup pot and bring to a simmer for 15
  minutes, or until potatoes are tender, and serve.

Goes well with *Mustard, Cheese, and Onion Popovers, page 197.*

Clam and Cheese Chowder

#1 Ingredients
4 cups fish or chicken stock
2 6-ounce cans chopped clams,
  with liquid
2 6-ounce cans minced clams,
  with liquid
1 cup potato, peeled and diced
  small
1/2 cup onion, diced small

1/2 cup celery, diced small
1/2 cup carrots, grated
1/4 cup fresh parsley, chopped
salt and white pepper to taste

#2 Ingredients
1 pint half-and-half
3 cups Colby cheese, shredded

Topper/croutons and chives

• Mix the #2 ingredients with a fork and set aside.
• Combine the #1 ingredients in a large soup pot and bring to a simmer for
  15 minutes. Slowly add the #2 ingredients, stirring constantly until the
  cheese is melted. Serve.

Goes well with *Sage and Onion Biscuits, page 169.*

New England Clam Chowder

about 6 16-ounce servings

#1 Ingredients
10 strips bacon, diced
1 cup onion, diced small

#2 Ingredients
4 cups fish or chicken
1 6-ounce bottle clam juice
1/2 cup celery, diced small
2 cups potato, peeled and diced
   small
salt and white pepper to taste

#3 Ingredient
2 pounds fresh baby clams, steamed
   and chopped, or 2 6-ounce
   cans whole clams with the
   liquid and 3 6-ounce cans
   chopped clams with the liquid

#4 Ingredients
1 cup half-and-half
1 cup sour cream

Topper/garlic croutons

- Mix the #4 ingredients and set aside.
- Fry and drain the #1 ingredients. Combine the #1 and #2 ingredients in a large soup pot and bring to a simmer for 20 minutes.
- Add the #3 ingredients and let continue to simmer another 5 minutes. Slowly add the #4 ingredients, stirring constantly until reheated. Serve.

Goes well with *Whole Wheat Quickbread*, page 163.

Variation: You can add 2 cups fresh sliced mushrooms with the #2 ingredients for a different flavor.

Hamaguri To Shiitake Ushiofiru

THE QUICK VERSION OF JAPANESE CLAM AND MUSHROOM SOUP

about 4 16-ounce servings

#1 Ingredients
6 cups fish or chicken stock
2 6-ounce cans chopped clams,
   with liquid
2 6-ounce cans minced clams,
   with liquid
1 cup fresh mushrooms, sliced

3 cups fresh spinach, packed and
   shredded
1/2 tablespoon fresh lemon zest
1 tablespoon soy sauce
white pepper to taste

Topper/green onions, sliced

- Combine the #1 ingredients in a large soup pot and bring to a simmer for 30 minutes. Serve.

Goes well with *Casserole Millet with Herbs*, page 159.

Shrimp Creole

about 6 16-ounce servings

#1 Ingredients
2 pounds shrimp, peeled and de-
veined
1 cup onion, diced small
1/4 teaspoon cayenne pepper or to
taste
1 tablespoon butter

1 14-ounce can stewed
tomatoes
1 large dried bay leaf
1/4 cup fresh parsley, chopped
1/2 cup green bell pepper,
chopped
salt and pepper to taste

#2 Ingredients
4 cups fish or chicken stock
2/3 cup celery, thinly sliced
2 cups fresh okra, sliced, or 2
cups sliced or cut frozen

#3 Ingredient
1/2 cup uncooked minute rice

Topper/garlic croutons and
shredded Colby cheese

- Saute the #1 ingredients and set aside.
- Combine the #2 ingredients in a large soup pot and bring to a simmer for 20 minutes. Add the #1 ingredients and let simmer for another 5 minutes. Add the #3 ingredient, and let rest for 5 minutes. Serve.

Goes well with *Cheesy Italian Popovers*, page 197.

Oriental Shrimp and Cabbage Soup

about 5 16-ounce servings

#1 Ingredients
6 cups fish or chicken stock
4 cups napa cabbage, chopped
and packed
1/2 cup celery, sliced at a slant 1/8
inch thick
1/2 cup green onions, sliced at a
slant 1/8 inch thick
2 tablespoons soy sauce

1 teaspoon fresh ginger,
minced
white pepper to taste

#2 Ingredient
2 pounds small shrimp, shelled
and de-veined

Topper/sliced green onions

- Combine the #1 ingredients in a large soup pot and bring to a simmer for 20 minutes. Add the #2 ingredient and continue to simmer for another 10 minutes, or until the shrimp have turned pink. Serve.

Goes well with *Tsung Yu Ping Flat Bread Chinese Onion Circles*, page 208.

Shrimp Gumbo

about 7 16-ounce servings

#1 Ingredients
6 cups fish or chicken stock
1 cup celery, sliced
1 cup onion, chopped
1 3-ounce jar chopped pimentos
   with liquid
1 tablespoon Italian seasoning
liquid cayenne pepper to taste
1 10-ounce package sliced or cut
   frozen okra, defrosted
salt to taste

#2 Ingredient
2 pounds shrimp, peeled and de-
   veined

#3 Ingredient
1/2 cup uncooked minute rice

Topper/Parmesan cheese and
   chives

- Combine the #1 ingredients in a large soup pot and bring to a simmer for 30 minutes. Add the #2 ingredient and continue to simmer for 10 minutes. Add the #3 ingredient and let rest for 5 minutes. Give a good stir and serve.

Goes well with *Parmesan Popovers*, page 197.

Scallop Stew

about 7 16-ounce servings

#1 Ingredients
1 pound scallops
1 tablespoon Worcestershire sauce

#2 Ingredients
6 cups fish or chicken
1/2 cup onion, diced small
salt and white pepper to taste

#3 Ingredients
1 pint half-and-half
2 cups longhorn cheese, shredded

Topper/several tiny shrimp
   sautéed in garlic powder and
   butter

- Mix the #3 ingredient with a wire whisk and set aside.
- Combine the #2 ingredients in a large soup pot and bring to a simmer for 20 minutes. Add the #1 ingredients, stirring very gently, and continue to simmer for 5 minutes. Slowly add the #3 ingredients, stirring gently and constantly until the cheese is melted. Serve.

Goes well with *Tiny Shrimp Biscuits*, page 172.

Curried Apple and Shrimp Soup

about 6 16-ounce servings

#1 Ingredients
6 cups chicken stock
1 large Granny Smith apple,
    peeled and diced small
1 cup celery, diced small
1 cup onion, diced small
1 cup potatoes, peeled and sliced
    thin
1/2 cup carrots, grated
salt and pepper to taste

#2 Ingredient
1 pound shrimp peeled and de-
    veined

#3 Ingredients
1 cup half-and-half
1 cup sour cream
2 tablespoons curry powder or to
    taste

Topper/sliced fresh chives

- Combine the #1 ingredients together in a large soup pot and bring to a simmer for 30 minutes, or until the apple is tender. Add the #2 ingredient and continue to simmer for another 10 minutes.
- Slowly add the #3 ingredients stirring constantly until reheated. Serve.

Goes well with *Mustardy Cheese Bread*, page 142.

Creamy Shrimp with Pasta

about 5 16-ounce servings

#1 Ingredients
6 cups fish or chicken stock
2 pounds shrimp, peeled and de-
    veined
1 teaspoon garlic, minced
2 tablespoon fresh basil, chopped
2 tablespoon fresh cilantro,
    chopped
1/4 cup carrots, grated
salt and pepper to taste

#2 Ingredient
2 handfuls uncooked curly pasta
    (fusilli)

#3 Ingredients
1 cup half-and-half
1 cup sour cream

Topper/Parmesan cheese

- Mix the #3 ingredients together with a wire whisk and set aside.
- Combine the #1 ingredients together in a large soup pot and bring to a simmer for 30 minutes. Add the #2 ingredient and continue to simmer for another 10 minutes. Slowly add the #3 ingredients, stirring constantly until reheated, and serve.

Goes well with *Onion Soup Mix Bread*, page 136.

Lobster Bisque

about 6 16-ounce servings

#1 Ingredients
6 cups fish or chicken stock
1 cup onion, diced small
1/2 cup carrots, grated
1 tablespoon butter
1/4 cup fresh parsley, chopped
1 teaspoon fresh tarragon, minced
1 teaspoon garlic, minced
1/8 teaspoon ground cayenne
    pepper, or to taste
1 16-ounce can stewed tomatoes,
    crushed and broken apart
salt to taste

#2 Ingredient
2 cups lobster meat

#3 Ingredients
1 cup heavy cream
1 cup sour cream

Topper/chives

- Mix the #3 ingredients together with a wire whisk and set aside.
- Combine the #1 ingredients in a large soup pot and bring to a simmer for 20 minutes. Add the #2 ingredient and continue to simmer for 5 minutes. Slowly add the #3 ingredients, stirring constantly until reheated. Serve.

Goes well with *Easy Popovers*, page 196.

Variations: You can use oysters instead of lobsters or just about any other shellfish. The list below will give you an idea of the cooking times. Let the #1 ingredients simmer for 20 minutes. Add the seafood and continue to cook with the following times given.

For oysters, cook 10 minutes
For scallops, cook 5 minutes
For shrimp, cook 10 minutes

For mussels, cook 10 minutes
For crabs, cook 10 minutes
For clams, cook 10 minutes

Creamy Mussel Stew

about 5 16-ounce servings

#1 Ingredients
4 cups fish or chicken stock
1 cup onion, chopped
1 tablespoon garlic, minced
1/4 cup fresh parsley,
    chopped
1 small dried bay leaf
1 tablespoon fresh thyme,
    minced
salt and pepper to taste

#2 Ingredients
1 pound shelled mussels, small or
    chopped
1 cup white wine

#3 Ingredients
1 cup half-and-half
1 cup sour cream

Topper/sliced green onions

- Mix the #2 ingredients with a wire whisk and set aside.
- Combine the #1 ingredients in a large soup pot and bring to a simmer for 20 minutes. Add the #2 ingredients and continue to simmer for 10 more minutes. Slowly add the #3 ingredients, stirring constantly until reheated. Serve.

Goes well with *Logan Bread*, page 165.

Oyster Chowder

about 6 16-ounce servings

#1 Ingredients
4 cups fish or chicken stock
8 slice bacons, diced
1 cup onion, chopped
1/2 cup celery, thinly sliced
2 16-ounce cans stewed tomatoes
6 tablespoons fresh parsley,
    chopped
1/4 teaspoon fresh thyme, chopped
1/8 teaspoon white pepper
1 cup potatoes, peeled and diced

#2 Ingredient
1 pound fresh shelled oysters, or 1
    10-ounce jar raw oysters (found
    in the refrigerated meat
    department)

#3 Ingredients
1 cup heavy cream
1 cup sour cream

Topper/sliced chives

- Mix the #3 ingredients together with a wire whisk and set aside.
- Combine the #1 ingredients together in a large soup pot and bring to a simmer for 30 minutes, or until the veggies are tender.
- Add the #2 ingredient and continue to simmer for another 5 minutes. Slowly add the #3 ingredients, stirring constantly until reheated, and serve.

Goes well with *Salt Buttermilk Biscuits*, page 175.

Oyster Stew

about 4 16-ounce servings

#1 Ingredients
4 cups fish or chicken stock
2 cups fresh oysters, or 1 10-ounce jar (found in the refrigerated meat department)
1 tablespoon dried onion flakes
1 small dried bay leaf
1/4 cup celery, thinly sliced
1 teaspoon garlic, minced
1/4 cup fresh parsley, chopped

1/8 teaspoon ground mace (optional)
salt and pepper to taste

#2 Ingredients
1 cup half-and-half
1 cup sherry (not cooking sherry)
1 cup sour cream

Topper/garlic croutons

- Mix the #2 ingredients together with a wire whisk and set aside.
- Combine the #1 ingredients in a large soup pot and bring to a simmer for 10 minutes. Slowly add the #2 ingredients, stirring constantly until reheated, and serve.

Goes well with *Onion Crackers*, page 201.

Crab Chowder

about 7 16-ounce servings

#1 Ingredients
1/2 cup onion, diced small
1 tablespoon butter
2 cups tomatoes, diced
1/2 cup celery, diced small
1/2 cup carrots, grated
1 cup fresh corn, cut off the cob, or 1 cup, frozen
1/4 cup fresh parsley, chopped
1/4 cup green bell pepper, diced small

#2 Ingredients
6 cups fish or chicken stock
4 cups crab meat
tabasco sauce to taste

Topper/you pick one!

- Sauté the #1 ingredients in a large soup pot. Add the #2 ingredients and bring to a simmer for 10 minutes. Serve.

Goes well with *Simple Biscuits*, page 167.

Good-Excuse-To-Eat-Shrimp Soup

about 7 16-ounce servings

#1 Ingredient
2 pounds shrimp, peeled and de-
veined

#2 Ingredients
4 cups fish or chicken stock
1/2 cup carrots, grated
1/2 teaspoon garlic, minced
1 cup fresh mushrooms, sliced
1/2 cup celery, sliced thin
1/4 cup green onion, sliced
2 14-ounce cans stewed tomatoes

1/3 cup fresh cilantro, chopped
salt and white pepper to taste

#3 Ingredients
1 cup half-and-half
2 cups jalapeño cheese, shredded
2 cups packed fresh spinach, or 1
10-ounce package frozen
spinach, chopped

Topper/diced avocado (good and
ripe)

- Mix the #3 ingredients with a fork and set aside.
- Combine the #2 ingredients in a large soup pot and bring to a simmer for
45 minutes. Add the #1 ingredient and continue to simmer for another 10
minutes, or until the shrimp turn pink.
- Slowly add the #3 ingredients, stirring constantly until the cheese is melted,
and serve.

Goes well with *Garlic Popovers*, page 197.

Haddie Chowder

about 6 16-ounce servings

#1 Ingredients
6 cups fish or chicken
2 tablespoons fresh parsley,
chopped
1 cup onion, chopped
2 cups potatoes, peeled and cut
into bite-sized pieces
1 small dried bay leaf
1 teaspoon ground paprika

#2 Ingredients
1 pound fresh haddock, cut into
bite-sized pieces
1/2 cup quick oatmeal
1 cup sherry or white wine

Topper/French fried onions

- Combine the #1 ingredients in a large soup pot and bring to a simmer for
30 minutes. Add the #2 ingredients and continue to simmer for 15 more
minutes. Serve.

Goes well with *Cheese and Onion Scones*, page 191.

Halibut with Saffron Soup

about 5 16-ounce servings

#1 Ingredients
4 cups fish or chicken stock
1 cup onion, chopped
2 cups tomatoes, diced
1/4 cup fresh parsley, chopped
3 tablespoons fresh chives, sliced
2 tablespoons fresh thyme, minced
1 small dried bay leaf
pinch of mace
pinch of saffron or to taste
1/2 cup red bell pepper, diced
    small
salt and pepper to taste

#2 Ingredient
1 pound halibut, cut into bite-sized
    pieces

#3 Ingredients
1 cup half-and-half
1 cup sour cream

Topper/garlic croutons

- Mix the #3 ingredients together with a wire whisk and set aside.
- Combine the #1 ingredients in a large soup pot and bring to a simmer for 20 minutes. Add the #2 ingredient and continue to simmer for another 10 minutes. Slowly add the #3 ingredients, stirring constantly until reheated, and serve.

Goes well with *Ham and Cheese Popovers*, page 197.

Scallop Stew

about 7 16-ounce servings

#1 Ingredients
1 pound scallops
1 tablespoon Worcestershire sauce

#2 Ingredients
6 cups fish or chicken
1/2 cup onion, diced small
salt and white pepper to taste

#3 Ingredients
1 pint half-and-half
2 cups longhorn cheese, shredded

Topper/several tiny shrimp
    sautéed in garlic powder and
    butter

- Mix the #3 ingredients with a wire whisk and set aside.
- Combine the #2 ingredients in a large soup pot and bring to a simmer for 20 minutes. Add the #1 ingredients, stirring very gently, and continue to simmer for 5 minutes. Slowly add the #3 ingredients, stirring gently and constantly until the cheese is melted. Serve.

Goes well with *Quick Cheese Bread*, page 136.

Salmon Chowder

about 6 16-ounce servings

#1 Ingredients
6 cups fish or chicken stock
1 cup onion, chopped
1/2 cup carrots, grated
1/2 cup celery, sliced thin
1 cup potatoes, diced small
1/8 teaspoon white pepper
1 cup mushrooms, sliced
1 teaspoon garlic, minced
1 tablespoon butter
salt and white pepper to taste

#2 Ingredient
2 cups salmon, diced

#3 Ingredients
1 cup heavy cream
1 cup sour cream

Topper/paprika and fresh sliced chives

- Mix the #3 ingredients together with a wire whisk and set aside.
- Combine the #1 ingredients in a large soup pot and bring to a simmer for 30 minutes. Add the #2 ingredient and continue to simmer for another 15 minutes. Slowly add the #3 ingredients, stirring constantly until reheated, and serve.

Goes well with *Cheese Popovers*, page 197.

Tuna, Pasta and Bean Soup

about 4 16-ounce servings

#1 Ingredients
4 cups chicken stock
2 6-ounce cans tuna, packed in
   water
1 15-ounce can pinto beans,
   drained
1/2 cup onion, chopped
1/2 cup carrots, grated
1 14-ounce can stewed tomatoes

#2 Ingredient
1 cup uncooked large elbow
   macaroni

Topper/chives

- Combine the #1 ingredients in a large soup pot and bring to a simmer for 30 minutes. Add the #2 ingredients and continue to simmer for 10 more minutes. Serve.

Goes well with *Tall Biscuits*, page 168.

Tuna and Tomato Soup with Cheese

about 7 16-ounce servings

#1 Ingredients
4 cups chicken stock
2 6-ounce cans tuna, in water
1 cup onion, diced small
2 cups potatoes, peeled and finely
  diced
1/2 cup carrots, grated
1 large dried bay leaf
2 14-ounce cans stewed tomatoes
1/4 cup fresh parsley, chopped
salt and pepper to taste

#2 Ingredients
1 cup half-and-half
1 cup sour cream
3 cups Monterey Jack cheese,
  shredded

Topper/diced red bell pepper

- Mix the #2 ingredients together with a fork and set aside.

- Combine the #1 ingredients in a large soup pot and bring to a simmer for 20 minutes. Slowly add the #2 ingredients, stirring constantly until the cheese is melted. Serve.

Goes well with *Cheese Popovers*, page 197.

Famous Cioppino

about 8 16-ounce servings

#1 Ingredients
3 cups chicken stock
2 14-ounce cans stewed tomatoes
1/2 cup zucchini, chopped
1/2 cup celery, thinly sliced
1/2 cup bell pepper, diced small
3 tablespoons dried onion flakes
1 cup onion, diced small
4 tablespoons fresh basil, chopped
1/2 tablespoon garlic, minced
1 small dried bay leaf
2 teaspoons fresh marjoram,
  minced, or 1 teaspoon, dried

1 teaspoon liquid cayenne pepper
1 cup fresh mushrooms, sliced
salt and white pepper to taste

#2 Ingredients
1/2 cup fresh lobster
1/2 cup fresh shrimp, peeled and
  de-veined
1/2 cup fresh small clams
1/2 cup fresh unshelled scallops
1/2 cup fresh unshelled mussels
1 cup sherry or dry white wine

- Combine the #1 ingredients in a large soup pot and bring to a simmer for 20 minutes. Add the #2 ingredients and continue to simmer for 10 minutes, or until the mussels and the clams open. Serve.

Goes well with *Sour Cream and Onion Loaf*, page 132.

Seafood Chowder

about 6 16-ounce servings

#1 Ingredients

4 cups fish or chicken stock
2 14-ounce cans stewed tomatoes
1 cup onion, chopped
1/2 cup celery, sliced
1 cup potato, peeled and diced
  small
1/2 cup carrots, grated
1 teaspoon garlic, minced
1 tablespoon fresh thyme, minced
1 small dried bay leaf
ground cayenne pepper to taste
1/2 tablespoon Old Bay seasoning
salt to taste

#2 Ingredients

1/2 cup halibut, cut into small
  pieces
1/2 cup raw oysters
1 cup small shrimp, peeled and
  de-veined
1/2 cup small fresh clams, shelled
1 cup crab meat, shredded

Topper/pat of butter

- Combine the #1 ingredients in a large soup pot and bring to a simmer for 20 minutes. Add the #2 ingredients and continue to simmer for another 10 minutes. Serve.

Goes well with *Loaded Cottage Cheese Buttermilk Biscuits*, page 177.

Variation: Add 1 cup half-and-half, 1 cup sour cream, and 2 cups of your favorite mild cheese, shredded. Mix ingredients first and set aside. After the soup has cooked, slowly add new ingredients, stirring constantly and gently until the cheese has melted.

New Orleans Seafood Gumbo

about 7 16-ounce servings

#1 Ingredients
4 cups fish or chicken stock
2 cups fresh mushrooms, sliced
1 cup onion, chopped
1 teaspoon fresh rosemary,
    chopped
1 tablespoon Worcestershire sauce
1/4 teaspoon fennel seed, ground
2 6-ounce bottles clam juice
2 cups fresh okra, sliced, or 1 10-
    ounce package sliced or cut
    frozen okra, defrosted
4 tablespoons fresh parsley,
    chopped

2/3 cup celery, diced small
1/2 cup carrots, grated
2 14-ounce cans stewed tomatoes
salt and white pepper to taste

#2 Ingredients
2 cups fresh crab meat, shredded
1/2 pound shrimp, peeled and
    de-veined
2 cups firm white fish, diced

Topper/tabasco sauce and red
    onions, diced

- Combine the #1 ingredients in a large soup pot and bring to a simmer for 30 minutes. Add the #2 ingredients and continue to simmer for another 10 minutes, or until the shrimp turns pink. Serve.

Goes well with *Tiny Shrimp Biscuits*, page 172.

Bouillabaisse

about 7 16-ounce servings

#1 Ingredients
6 cups fish or chicken stock
1/2 cup carrots, diced small
1/2 cup onion, chopped
1/4 cup leeks, thinly sliced (whites only)
2 cups tomatoes, diced
3 teaspoons garlic, minced
1 tablespoon fresh fennel, minced
1 teaspoon orange zest
2 small dried bay leaves
1 tablespoon tomato paste
1/4 teaspoon celery seed
1/4 cup fresh parsley, chopped

1 teaspoon fresh thyme, minced
1/4 teaspoon saffron strands
salt and pepper to taste

#2 Ingredients
1 pound shrimp, shelled
1 pound white fish, cut into bite-sized pieces
1 cup lobster meat, cut into bite-sized pieces
1/2 pound fresh clams in the shell

Topper/melted butter for dipping

- Combine the #1 ingredients in a large soup pot and bring to a simmer for 30 minutes. Add the #2 ingredients to the #1 ingredients and let simmer 5 to 10 minutes or until the clams open. Serve.

Goes well with *Sesame Seed Crackers*, page 201.

Chapter 10

CREAM SOUPS AND CHEESE SOUPS

Just a quick reminder: I personally never use heavy cream or even half-and-half, unless it is a special occasion. I use 1% milk and low-fat sour cream, and still get that creamy taste. I wanted to give the original recipe and let you make the decision whether or not you wanted a low-fat meal. Check the no-fat sour creams and cheeses. Some products do not recommend that you cook with them. I have found low-fat cheeses work quite well when melting in soups.

If you are on a no-fat diet there is a quick tip in the *All Kinds of Tips* chapter, page 5, on how to use canned navy beans, and still get creamy results.

Also for those of you trying to cut back on fats, you can leave out the milk products and put the cooked soup in the blender and blend until smooth. Add a pat of low-fat margarine or a low-fat shredded cheese as a topper and have a wonderful tasting soup. All blender soups will be indicated in the **Variations** on page 97.

French Cream of Lettuce Soup
about 3 16-ounce servings

#1 Ingredients
4 cups chicken stock
1 head of Boston lettuce, shredded
1/2 cup onion, diced small
1 tablespoon butter
salt and white pepper to taste

#2 Ingredients
2 cups half-and-half
1/2 teaspoon fresh mint leaves, minced

Topper/few fresh mint leaves

- Mix the #2 ingredients with a wire whisk and set aside.
- Combine the #1 ingredients in a large soup pot and bring to a simmer for 20 minutes. Slowly add the #2 ingredients, stirring constantly until reheated, and serve.

Goes well with *Ham and Cheese Biscuits*, page 172.

Cream of Broccoli

THIS IS A BASIC CREAM SOUP RECIPE.
TO USE OTHER INGREDIENTS SEE **VARIATIONS**.

about 4 16-ounce servings

#1 Ingredients
4 cups chicken stock
2 cups broccoli, chopped small, or
    1-10 ounce package, frozen
    and chopped
1 cup celery, sliced thin
1/2 cup onion, diced small

1/2 teaspoon Worcestershire sauce
salt and white pepper to taste

#2 Ingredients
1 cup half-and-half
1 cup sour cream

Topper/Colby cheese, shredded

- Mix the #2 ingredients with a wire whisk and set aside.
- Combine the #1 ingredients in a large soup pot and bring to a simmer for 15 minutes. Slowly add the #2 ingredients, stirring constantly until reheated. Serve.

Goes well with *Sage Corn Bread*, page 185.

Cream of Tomato with Basil

BLENDER SOUP

about 6 16-ounce servings

#1 Ingredients
1 cup chicken stock
4 14-ounce cans stewed tomatoes,
    diced
1/2 cup onion, diced small
4 tablespoons fresh basil, minced
salt and pepper to taste

#2 Ingredients
1 pint half-and-half
1 cup sour cream

Topper/buttered popcorn

- Mix the #2 ingredients together with a wire whisk and set aside.
- Combine the #1 ingredients in a large soup pot and bring to a simmer for 20 minutes. Slowly add the #2 ingredients, stirring constantly until reheated, and serve.

Goes well with *Quick Pumpernickel*, page 160.

Variations:

Just switch the vegetable, or main ingredient, using the following directions:

INGREDIENTS	AMOUNT	COOKING TIMES	
Artichoke hearts	2 cups, diced small	15 minutes	Blender soup
Asparagus	2 cups, tips only	5 to 10 minutes	Blender soup
Brussel Sprouts	2 cups, chopped and packed	15 minutes	Blender soup
Cabbage	2 cups, chopped and packed	15 minutes	Blender soup
Cauliflower	2 cups florets	15 minutes	Blender soup
Celery	2 cups, thinly sliced	15 to 20 minutes	Blender soup
Chicken	2 cups, diced	20 minutes	
Corn	2 cups, fresh, cut off cob or frozen	10 minutes	
Ham (smoked)	2 cups, diced small	15 minutes	
Hubbard squash	2 cups, peeled and diced small	15 minutes	Blender soup
Lima Beans	2 cups, fresh or frozen	20 minutes	
Mushrooms	2 cups, fresh, sliced	10 minutes	
Onion	1 cup, diced small	20 minutes	
Peas, Carrots or Pearl Onions	2 cups	15 minutes or 20 minutes for pearl onions	Blender soup
Potato, or Potatoes and Chives	2 cups, peeled and diced small	15 minutes	Blender soup
Spinach	2 cups, chopped and packed	10 minutes	Blender soup
Water cress	2 cups, chopped and packed	10 minutes	Blender soup
Yellow Squash	2 cups, peeled and diced small	10 minutes	Blender soup
Zucchini	2 cups, diced small	15 minutes	Blender soup

Variations:

INGREDIENTS	AMOUNT	COOKING TIME
Beef	2 cups, diced small	15 minutes
Broccoli	4 cups fresh florets or 2 10-ounce, frozen	10 minutes
Chicken	2 cups, diced small	15 minutes
Corn	4 cups, cut off the cob or 4 cups frozen	10 minutes
Ham	2 cups, diced small	15 minutes
Onion	2 cups, diced small	20 minutes
Other cheeses: such as Monterey Jack, Longhorn, Cheddar, Etc.	3 cups cheese	Follow recipe directions.
Pepperoni	1 cup, diced small and cooked before adding	10 minutes
Spinach	4 cups, packed or 2 10-ounce frozen	10 minutes
Tuna	2 6-ounce cans drained	10 minutes

Cheese Pimento Soup

about 5 16-ounce servings

#1 Ingredients
4 cups chicken stock
1 cup ham, diced small
1 cup onion, diced small
1/2 cup carrots, grated
1/2 cup celery, diced small
1 3-ounce jar pimentos, chopped
salt and white pepper to taste

#2 Ingredients
2 8-ounce jars pimento cheese
1 pint of half-and-half
1 cup sour cream

Topper/sliced green olives

• Using an electric mixer, mix the #2 ingredients together and set aside.
• Combine the #1 ingredients together in a large soup pot and bring to a simmer for 20 minutes. Slowly add the #2 ingredients, stirring constantly until reheated and serve.

Goes well with *Pickle in a Loaf*, page 131.

Yellow Tomato Bisque

about 7 16-ounce servings

#1 Ingredients
4 cups chicken stock
4 cups golden or yellow-boy
  tomatoes, diced
1 cup onion, chopped
1/2 cup celery, sliced
1/2 cup carrots, grated
1 teaspoon garlic, minced
2 tablespoons sugar
1 teaspoon fresh oregano,
  minced, or 1/2 teaspoon dried
  oregano flakes

1 tablespoon fresh cilantro,
  minced
salt and white pepper to taste

#2 Ingredients
1 cup half-and-half
1 cup sour cream

Topper/diced red bell pepper

- Mix the #2 ingredients together with a wire whisk and set aside.
- Combine the #1 ingredients in a large soup pot and bring to a simmer for 1 hour. Using a blender, blend until smooth. Return to a low heat and slowly add the #2 ingredients, stirring constantly until reheated, and serve.

Goes well with *Paraguay Corn Loaf*, page 189.

Cauliflower and Cheese

THIS IS A BASIC CHEESE SOUP RECIPE. TO USE DIFFERENT INGREDIENTS SEE VARIATIONS AT THE END OF THIS RECIPE.

about 6 16-ounce servings

#1 Ingredients
4 cups chicken stock
4 cups fresh cauliflower florets, or
  2 10-ounce frozen packages,
  defrosted
1/2 cup onion, diced small
1/2 cup carrots, grated
salt and pepper to taste

#2 Ingredients
1 pint heavy cream
1 cup sour cream
3 cups American or Colby cheese,
  shredded

Topper/melba rounds

- Mix the #2 ingredients together with a wire whisk and set aside.
- Combine the #1 ingredients in a large soup pot and bring to a simmer for 20 minutes. Add the #2 ingredients, stirring constantly until the cheese is melted and serve.

Goes well with *Onion and Parmesan Buttermilk Biscuits*, page 178.

Chili Con Queso Soup

about 6 16-ounce servings

#1 Ingredients
4 cups chicken stock
1 cup onion, chopped
1/2 cup carrots, grated
1 3-ounce canned green chilies,
  chopped
1 cup fresh mushrooms, sliced
1 cup frozen corn
salt and white pepper to taste

#2 Ingredients
3 cups Monterey Jack cheese,
  shredded
1 cup heavy cream
1 cup sour cream
1 teaspoon ground cumin
2 cups tomatoes, diced

Topper/diced red bell pepper and
chives

- Mix the #2 ingredients with a fork and set aside.
- Combine the #1 ingredients in a large soup pot and bring to a simmer for 20 minutes. Slowly add the #2 ingredients, stirring constantly and gently until the cheese is melted. Serve.

Goes well with *Frito Corn Bread*, page 187.

Potato Cheese Chowder

about 5 16-ounce servings

#1 Ingredients
4 cups chicken stock
2 cups potatoes, peeled and diced
  small
1/2 cup green bell pepper, diced
  small
1/2 cup onion, diced small
1/4 cup fresh parsley, chopped
1 tablespoon butter
salt and pepper to taste

#2 Ingredients
1 pint half-and-half
1 cup sour cream
3 cups Colby cheese, shredded

Topper/bacon bits

- Mix the #2 ingredients with a fork and set aside.
- Combine the #1 ingredients in a large soup pot, and bring to a simmer for 25 minutes. Slowly add the #2 ingredients and stir constantly until reheated. Serve.

Goes well with *Buckwheat and Sesame Seed Quickbread*, page 161.

Creamy Potato and Dill Soup

about 6 16-ounce servings

#1 Ingredients
4 cups chicken stock
2 cups smoked ham, cut into bite-
sized pieces
4 cups potatoes, peeled and diced
1/2 cup onion, diced
1/2 cup celery, diced
2 tablespoons fresh dill weed
salt and pepper to taste

#2 Ingredients
1 cup heavy cream
1 cup sour cream

Topper/pat of butter with sliced
fresh chives

- Mix the #2 ingredients with a wire whisk and set aside.
- Combine the #1 ingredients in a large soup pot and bring to a simmer for 30 minutes. Slowly add the #2 ingredients, stirring constantly until reheated and serve.

Goes well with *Herb and Onion Loaf*, page 131.

Macaroni and Cheese with Olives Soup

about 6 16-ounce servings

#1 Ingredients
6 cups chicken stock
1/2 cup green olives, chopped
1/2 cup black olives, sliced
2 tablespoons pimento, chopped
1/2 cup onion, diced small
2 tablespoons red bell pepper,
diced small
salt and pepper to taste

#3 Ingredients
1 pint half-and-half
1 cup sour cream
2 cups Monterey Jack cheese,
shredded

Topper/garlic melba rounds,
crumbled

#2 Ingredient
1 cup small-shell pasta

- Mix the #3 ingredients using a fork and set aside.
- Combine the #1 ingredients in a large soup pot and bring to a simmer for 20 minutes. Add the #2 ingredient and continue to simmer until the pasta is tender. Slowly add the #3 ingredients, stirring constantly until the cheese is melted and serve.

Goes well with *Cheese and Cayenne Drop Biscuits*, page 181.

Russian Cabbage Soup

about 8 16-ounce servings

#1 Ingredients
6 cups beef stock
2 cups smoked turkey, finely
    diced
1/2 cup carrots, diced small
1 cup potatoes, peeled and diced
    small
1/2 cup celery, diced small
1 cup tomatoes, diced small
1 tablespoon fresh dill weed

1/2 cup onion, chopped
2 cups cabbage, shredded and
    packed
salt and pepper to taste

#2 Ingredients
1 cup half-and-half
2 cups sour cream

Topper/diced avocado

- Mix the #2 ingredients with a wire whisk and set aside.
- Combine the #1 ingredients in a large soup pot and bring to a simmer for 20 minutes. Slowly add the #2 ingredients stirring constantly, until reheated and serve.

Goes well with *Dill and Mustard Drop Biscuits*, page 181.

Potato Kielbasa Cheese Chowder

about 6 16-ounce servings

#1 Ingredients
6 cups chicken stock
4 cups kielbasa sausage, cut into
    bite-sized pieces
2 cups potatoes, peeled and diced
    small
1 cup onion, diced small
1/4 cup fresh parsley, chopped
salt and white pepper to taste

#2 Ingredients
1 pint half-and-half
2 cups Colby cheese, shredded

Topper/sliced green onion

- Mix the #2 ingredients together and set aside.
- Combine the #1 ingredients together in a large soup pot and bring to a simmer for 30 minutes. Slowly add the #2 ingredients, stirring constantly until the cheese is melted and serve.

Goes well with *Quickbread with Dill*, page 125.

Turkish Buttermilk Soup

about 5 16-ounce servings

#1 Ingredients
6 cups chicken stock
1 cup onion, chopped
1 teaspoon fresh dill weed
1 tablespoon butter
1/2 cup quick cooking barley
salt and pepper to taste

#2 Ingredient
2 cups buttermilk

Topper/garlic melba rounds

- Combine the #1 ingredients in a large soup pot and bring to a simmer for 30 minutes. Slowly add the #2 ingredient, stirring constantly until reheated and serve.

Goes well with *Onion and Parmesan Buttermilk Biscuits*, page 178.

September Soup

about 7 16-ounce servings

#1 Ingredient
8 slices bacon, diced

#2 Ingredients
6 cups chicken stock
1/2 cup green onion, sliced
1/2 cup carrots, diced small
1 cup stalk celery, diced small
2 cups potatoes, peeled and diced
1 cup fresh green beans, cut and
   tips removed

1 cup corn, cut off the cob
2 tablespoons fresh marjoram,
   minced
salt and pepper to taste

#3 Ingredient
1/2 cup uncooked minute rice

#4 Ingredient
1 pint half-and-half

- Fry and drain the #1 ingredients, combine the #1 and #2 ingredients in a large soup pot, and bring to a simmer for 20 minutes. Add the #3 ingredients and wait 5 minutes.
- Slowly add the #4 ingredients, stirring constantly until reheated, and serve.

Goes well with *Ham and Cheese Popovers*, page 197.

Creamy Tuna Curry Soup

about 5 16-ounce servings

#1 Ingredients
6 cups chicken stock
2 6-ounce cans tuna in spring
water with liquid
1/2 cup onion, finely chopped
1 tablespoon curry powder
1 tablespoon butter
1/2 teaspoon fresh lemon zest
salt and pepper to taste

#2 Ingredients
1 pint half-and-half
2 cups sour cream

Topper/shredded Monterey Jack
cheese

- Mix the #2 ingredients with a wire whisk and set aside.
- Combine the #1 ingredients in a large soup pot and bring to a simmer for 20 minutes. Slowly add the #2 ingredients, stirring constantly until reheated and serve.

Goes well with *Poppy and Parmesan Cheese Bread Sticks*, page 199.

Stracciatella

ITALIAN EGG AND CHEESE SOUP

about 4 16-ounce servings

#1 Ingredients
6 cups chicken stock
2 tablespoons fresh parsley,
chopped

#2 Ingredients
3/4 cup uncooked acini de pepe
pasta (sometimes called
peppercorn pasta)

#3 Ingredient
1 egg, well beaten

#4 Ingredient
1/2 cup Parmesan cheese

- Combine the #1 ingredients in a large soup pot and bring to a boil. Add the #2 ingredients and simmer until the pasta is done.
- Slowly drizzle in the #3 ingredient and remove from the heat. Add the #4 ingredient, give a good stir, and serve.

Goes well with *Garlic Loaf*, page 127.

Cheese and Beer Soup

about 4 16-ounce servings

#1 Ingredients
1 cup beef stock
1/2 cup onion, diced small
3 tablespoons butter
1/2 teaspoon dry mustard
1/2 cup carrots, grated
salt and pepper to taste

#2 Ingredient
2 12-ounce cans of your favorite
   beer

#3 Ingredient
4 cups Colby cheese, grated

Topper/black olives, sliced

- Combine the #1 ingredients in a large soup pot and bring to a simmer for 10 minutes. Add the #2 ingredients and give a good stir. Add the #3 ingredients, stirring constantly until the cheese is melted, and serve.

Goes well with *Cheese and Cayenne Drop Biscuits*, page 181.

Creamy Chip Beef Chowder

about 5 16-ounce servings

#1 Ingredients
4 cups beef stock
2 5-ounce jar dried chipped beef,
   diced small
2 cups potatoes, peeled and diced
   small
1/2 cup onion, chopped
1/2 cup carrots, grated
1/2 cup celery, diced small
1/2 cup bell pepper, diced small
salt and pepper to taste

#2 Ingredient
1 cup milk

#3 Ingredients
3 tablespoons onion, minced
3 tablespoons butter

#4 Ingredient
1/3 cup all-purpose flour

Topper/mild cheddar cheese,
   shredded

- Sauté the #3 ingredients until the onion are transparent and set aside, leaving the ingredients in the pan.
- Combine the #1 ingredients in a large soup pot and bring to a simmer for 20 minutes. Add the #2 ingredient and continue to simmer for 5 minutes.
- Reheat the #3 ingredients, add the #4 ingredient and stir until flour is well absorbed and smooth. (You have just made a roux). Add to the #1 ingredients stirring until thickened. Serve.

Goes well with *Tall Biscuits*, page 168.

Creamy Herbed Beef Stew

about 9 16-ounce servings

#1 Ingredients
6 cups beef stock
2 cups stew meat, cut into small bite-sized pieces
1/2 cup zucchini, diced small
1/2 cup frozen baby lima beans
1/2 cup celery, sliced thin
2 cups potato, peeled and diced small
1/2 cup green bell pepper, chopped small
1/2 cup carrots, sliced thin
1/2 cup turnip, peeled and diced small
1/2 cup frozen corn
1 1/2 teaspoon garlic, minced
1 large dried bay leaf

2 14-ounce cans stewed tomatoes
1 teaspoon onion powder or to taste
1 teaspoon garlic powder or to taste
3 tablespoons fresh basil, minced
1 tablespoon fresh oregano, minced
1/2 tablespoon fresh thyme, chopped
1 teaspoon paprika
salt and pepper to taste

#2 Ingredients
1 cup half-and-half
2 cups sour cream

- Mix the #2 ingredients together with a wire whisk and set aside.
- Combine the #1 ingredients in a large soup pot and bring to a simmer for 30 minutes. Slowly add the #2 ingredients, stirring constantly until reheated, and serve.

Goes well with *Garlic Popovers*, page 197.

Virginia Peanut Butter Soup

about 5 16-ounce servings

#1 Ingredients
6 cups chicken stock
1/2 cup onion, chopped
1/2 cup celery, diced small
salt and pepper to taste

#2 Ingredients
1 pint heavy cream
1 cup creamy peanut butter

Topper/chopped roasted peanuts

- Using an electric mixer, mix the #2 ingredients until well blended and set aside.
- Combine the #1 ingredients in a large soup pot and bring to a simmer for 30 minutes. Slowly add the #2 ingredients, stirring constantly until reheated, and serve.

Goes well with *Banana Orange Nut Loaf*, page 152.

Cream of Hamburger with Pasta

about 6 16-ounce servings

#1 Ingredients
1 pound hamburger
1 cup onions, chopped

#2 Ingredients
6 cups beef stock
1 cup celery, diced small
2 14-ounce cans stewed tomatoes
1/4 cup parsley, chopped
1 teaspoon fresh oregano, minced
1 teaspoon garlic, minced
1 teaspoon fresh basil, minced
salt and pepper to taste

#3 Ingredient
1/2 cup stelline, or stellette pasta
 (star)

#4 Ingredients
1 cup half-and-half
1 cup sour cream

Topper/Romano cheese, grated

- Brown and drain the #1 ingredients.
- Mix the #4 ingredients and set aside.
- Combine the #1 and #2 ingredients in a large soup pot and bring to a simmer for 30 minutes. Add the #3 ingredient and continue to simmer for another 5 minutes or until the pasta is cooked. Slowly add the #4 ingredients, stirring constantly until reheated and serve.

Goes well with *Onion Soup Mix Loaf*, page 136.

Bacon and Cheese Soup

about 5 16-ounce servings

#1 Ingredient
12 strips bacon, diced

#2 Ingredients
4 cups chicken stock
1 cup onion, finely diced

#3 Ingredients
1 pint half-and-half
1 cup sour cream
3 cups American cheese, diced
 small

Topper/chives

- Brown the #1 ingredient and drain.
- Mix the #3 ingredients together with a fork and set aside.
- Combine the #1 and the #2 ingredients in a large soup pot and bring to a simmer for 30 minutes. Slowly add the #3 ingredients, stirring constantly until the cheese is melted and serve.

Goes well with *Sesame and Onion Drop Biscuits*, page 181.

Another Cheese and Beer Soup But Different

about 5 16-ounce servings

#1 Ingredients
4 cups chicken stock
2 tablespoons butter
1/2 cup onion, diced small
1/2 cup carrots, grated
1/2 cup celery, diced small
1/4 cup green bell pepper, diced
   small
1 3-ounce jar pimentos, chopped
salt and pepper to taste

#2 Ingredient
3 cups Monterey Jack cheese

#3 Ingredient
1 12-ounce can of your favorite
   beer

Topper/garlic croutons

• Combine the #1 ingredients in a large soup pot and bring to a simmer for 20 minutes. Add the #3 ingredient and reheat. Add the #2 ingredient, stirring constantly until the cheese melts, and serve.

Goes well with *Buttery Beer Bread*, page 133.

Cheesy Ham and Dill Soup

about 8 16-ounce servings

#1 Ingredients
4 cups chicken stock
4 cups smoked ham, cut into bite-
   sized pieces
1 cup onion, chopped
1/2 cup celery, sliced thin
2 cups potatoes, peeled and diced
   small
1/2 cup carrots, grated
1/4 cup green bell pepper, diced
   small
3 tablespoons dill weed
salt and pepper to taste

#2 Ingredients
1 pint half-and-half
1 cup sour cream
3 cups mild cheddar

Topper/sour cream and dill

• Mix the #2 ingredients and set aside.
• Combine the #1 ingredients in a large soup pot and bring to a simmer for 30 minutes. Slowly add the #2 ingredients, stirring constantly until the cheese is melted, and serve.

Goes well with *French Fried Onion Biscuits*, page 169.

Chapter 11

COLD SOUPS

For the cold soups (that you don't cook, then chill), it is a good idea to start off with ice cold ingredients.

Cold Cucumber Soup
about 5 16-ounce servings

#1 Ingredients
4 cups chicken stock
4 cups cucumber, peeled,
    chopped, and seeded
1/4 cup green onions, sliced thin
1 teaspoon fresh dill weed
salt and white pepper to taste

#2 Ingredients
1 pint half-and-half
1 cup sour cream

Topper/thinly sliced cucumber

- Combine the #1 ingredients in a large soup pot and bring to a simmer for 30 minutes. Chill completely.
- Using a blender, blend the #1 ingredients until smooth. Mix the #2 ingredients with a wire whisk and add to the #1 ingredients and continue to blend until smooth. Serve.

Goes well with *Celery and Onion Bread*, page 136.

Indian Cool Mint
about 2 16-ounce servings

#1 Ingredients
4 cups plain yogurt
2 large cucumbers peeled, seeded,
    and chopped
4 tablespoons fresh mint leaves,
    chopped

1 teaspoon sugar
salt and white pepper to taste

Topper/mint leaves

- Combine the #1 ingredients in a blender and blend until smooth. Chill completely and serve.

Goes well with *Chapati Indian Flat Bread*, page 206.

Cold Spinach Soup

about 3 16-ounce servings

#1 Ingredients
2 cups chicken stock
2 10-ounce packages frozen,
   chopped spinach, defrosted
   with the water squeezed out
   (use your hands)
1/4 cup onion, chopped
salt and pepper to taste

#2 Ingredients
1 pint half-and-half
1 cup sour cream

Topper/sour cream and fresh
   chives, sliced

• Using a blender, blend the #1 ingredients until smooth.
• Add the #2 ingredients and continue to blend until well mixed. Chill and serve.

Goes well with *Sun-Dried Tomato and Onion Buttermilk Biscuits*, page 179.

Cold Apple Buttermilk with Curry Soup

about 4 16-ounce servings

#1 Ingredients
2 cups chicken stock
2 cups red delicious apples, diced
   small, with skins left on for
   color and sweetness
1/4 cup onion, diced small
1/4 teaspoon curry powder, or to
   taste

1/8 teaspoon mustard seed
2 cups apple sauce
salt and pepper to taste

#2 Ingredient
2 cups buttermilk

Topper/toasted almond slivers

• Combine the #1 ingredients and bring to a simmer for 10 minutes. Then using a blender, blend until smooth. Add the #2 ingredient and continue to blend until well mixed. Chill and serve.

Goes well with *Sweet Little Honey Puffs*, page 205.

Vichyssoise

about 4 16-ounce servings

#1 Ingredients
4 cups chicken stock
1/2 cup onion, diced small
1/2 cup celery, diced small
1/4 cup parsley, diced small
2 cups potatoes, peeled and diced
small
1 cup leeks, thinly sliced (white
parts only)
1 tablespoon butter
salt and white pepper to taste

#2 Ingredient
1 pint heavy cream

Topper/fresh chives

- Combine the #1 ingredients in a large soup pot and bring to a simmer for 30 minutes, chill completely.
- Using a blender, blend the #1 ingredients until smooth. Slowly add the #2 ingredients continuing to blend until well mixed. Serve.

Goes well with *Quick Onion Rye with Caraway Seeds*, page 159.

Gazpacho

about 5 16-ounce servings

#1 Ingredients
6 cups spicy V-8 (spicy, optional)
6 large ripe tomatoes, diced
2 large cucumbers, peeled,
seeded, and diced
1 cup onion, diced
1/4 cup green bell pepper,
chopped
1/2 cup red wine
1/2 cup carrots, grated

2 teaspoons garlic, minced
1 tablespoon olive oil
tabasco sauce to taste
1/2 teaspoon Worcestershire sauce
6 ice cubes
salt and pepper to taste

Topper/sour cream and fresh
chives

- Using a blender, blend until smooth, chill, and serve.

Goes well with *Onion and Dill Bread*, page 136.

Cold Guacamole Soup

IF YOU LIKE GUACAMOLE DIP YOU'LL LIKE THIS SOUP

about 4 16-ounce servings

#1 Ingredients
2 cups chicken stock (cold)
4 very ripe avocados, peeled and diced
4 tablespoons onion, diced small
1 teaspoon liquid cayenne pepper, or to taste
1 pint half-and-half
1 cup sour cream
salt and pepper to taste

#2 Ingredients
2 cup tomatoes, diced
¼ cup green onion, sliced thin

Topper/tortilla chips with shredded cheddar

• Using a blender, blend the #1 ingredients until smooth. Fold in the #2 ingredients, and serve.

Goes well with *French Fried Onion Biscuits*, page 169.

Cold Spanish Veggie Soup

about 6 16-ounce servings

#1 Ingredients
4 cups spicy V-8 (spicy optional)
4 cups tomatoes, diced small
½ cup green bell peppers, chopped
½ cup celery, sliced thin
1 teaspoon garlic, minced
½ cup carrots, grated
1 cup onion, diced small
1 cup fresh corn, cut off the cob or 1 cup frozen
1 cup green onions, sliced thin
1 tablespoon vinegar
2 tablespoons fresh cilantro, chopped
1 tablespoon Worcestershire sauce
liquid cayenne pepper to taste

Topper/pat of butter and small red bell pepper, diced

• Combine in a large bowl, give a good stir and chill until serving time.

Goes well with *Chili Crackers*, page 200.

Beef or Chicken Consommé

A CLEAR BROTH THAT CAN BE SERVED HOT OR COLD

- Follow the same recipes for the stocks on page 8, and you have consommé. Some people like adding tomato juice to the beef consommé: To 6 cups of consommé, add 1 cup tomato juice and simmer for 15 minutes. Serve.

Chilled Cherry Soup

about 4 16-ounce servings

#1 Ingredients
4 cups apple juice
2 16-ounce cans tart pitted
 cherries, with liquid
1/2 cup sugar
2 tablespoons fresh lemon juice
1/2 teaspoon anise seeds, crushed

Topper/sour cream with canned mandarin orange slices

- Combine the #1 ingredients in a medium soup pot and bring to a simmer just until the sugar melts. Using a blender, blend until smooth, chill completely, and serve.

Goes well with *Butterscotch Tea Bread*, page 157.

Cool Pear Soup

about 5 16-ounce servings

#1 Ingredients
1 cup apple juice
2 16-ounce cans pears in syrup
 with liquid
1 cup half-and-half
1 cup vanilla ice cream

#2 Ingredient
1 cup chunky apple sauce

Topper/whipped cream with fresh berries

- Using a blender, blend the #1 ingredients until smooth and stir in the #2 ingredient. Serve.

Goes well with *Boston Brown Bread*, page 165.

Cold Peach Berry Soup

about 5 16-ounce servings

#1 Ingredients
2 cups orange juice
3 cups fresh blueberries, or 3 cups
  frozen
2 16-ounce cans peaches, with
  juice
½ cup sugar or to taste

#2 Ingredient
1 pint half-and-half

Topper/whipped cream

• Combine the #1 ingredients in a medium soup pot and bring to a simmer for 10 minutes. Chill completely.
• Using a blender, blend the #1 ingredients until smooth. Slowly add the #2 ingredients, blend until well mixed, and serve.

Goes well with *Lemon Poppy Bread*, page 146.

Mixed Cold Fruit Soup

about 4 16-ounce servings

#1 Ingredients
2 cups orange juice
1 cup half-and-half
1 cup vanilla ice cream
2 16-ounce cans fruit cocktail,
  with the liquid
1 6-ounce jar cherries

Topper/sour cream with a few
  berries (your choice)

• Combine the #1 ingredients in a blender, blend until smooth and serve.

Goes well with *Orange Spice Bread*, page 147.

Cream of Almond Soup

about 4 16-ounce servings

#1 Ingredients
1 cup milk
1 cup sour cream
2 cups vanilla ice cream
1 pint half-and-half

2 cups toasted almond slivers
1 teaspoon almond extract
1/4 cup sugar

Topper/toasted almond slivers

• Using a blender, blend the #1 ingredients until smooth. Serve.

Goes well with *Lemony Almond Bread*, page 148.

Cold Santa Fe Melon Soup

about 3 16-ounce servings

#1 Ingredients
1 pint half-and-half
2 cups milk
1/2 cup vanilla ice cream
4 cups ripe cantaloupes, chilled,
   seeded, and diced

1 tablespoon sugar
4 fresh mint leaves, chopped

Topper/vanilla ice cream with
   fresh mint leaves

• Using a blender, blend the #1 ingredients until smooth and serve.

Goes well with *Rich Chocolate Scones*, page 191.

Kiwi Soup with Mint

THIS IS A WONDERFUL COLD DESERT SOUP FOR A HOT SUMMER NIGHT

about 3 16-ounce servings

#1 Ingredients
1 cup apricot nectar
1 pint half-and-half
2 cups sour cream
6 kiwi fruits, diced, with the pulp
   removed
5 large fresh mint leaves
1/2 cup sugar

Topper/thinly sliced orange slices

• Using a blender, blend the #1 ingredients until smooth. Serve.

Goes well with *New England Banana Bread*, page 151.

Just Peachy Cold Soup with a Kick

about 3 16-ounce servings

#1 Ingredients
2 cups apple juice
1 pint half-and-half
1/4 cup peach liqueur
4 cups fresh, ripe peaches, peeled
    and sliced

Topper/whipped cream with a
    mint leaf

• Combine the #1 ingredients in a blender, blend until smooth and serve.

Goes well with *Best Ever Chocolate Tea Bread*, page 157.

Cold Apple Cinnamon Soup

about 4 16-ounce servings

#1 Ingredients
4 cups apple sauce
1 teaspoon cinnamon
1/2 cup sugar
1 pint half-and-half
1 cup milk

#2 Ingredient
2 large red delicious apples, finely
    diced (with skin on)

Topper/vanilla ice cream with
    cinnamon sugar

• Mix the #1 ingredients. Add the #2 ingredient, give a good stir, and serve.

Goes well with *Lemony Almond Bread*, page 148.

Cold Scandinavian Raspberry Soup

about 3 16-ounce servings

#1 Ingredients
4 cups orange juice
1 tablespoon lemon juice
1 cup sweet white wine
2 cups fresh ripe raspberries, or 2
    cups frozen

Topper/mandarin orange slices

• Using a blender, blend the #1 ingredients together until smooth, and serve.

Goes well with *Whole Wheat Honey Bread*, page 161.

Cold Rhubarb and Strawberry Soup

about 4 16-ounce servings

#1 Ingredients
2 cups apple juice
2 cups orange juice
2 cups fresh rhubarb, diced
3/4 cup sugar

#2 Ingredient
2 cups fresh, ripe strawberries, or
  2 cups frozen strawberries,
  defrosted

Topper/whipped cream and
  canned mandarin orange slices

- Combine the #1 ingredients together in a medium soup pot and bring to a simmer for 15 minutes, or until the rhubarb is tender. Chill completely.
- Using a blender, blend the #1 and #2 ingredients together until smooth, and serve.

Goes well with *John's Gumdrop Bread*, page 158.

Cold Apricot Soup

about 4 16-ounce servings

#1 Ingredients
1 pint half-and-half
2 16-ounce cans apricots, with
  liquid
1 tablespoon sugar
2 cups vanilla ice cream
1/8 teaspoon cinnamon

Topper/sprinkle of cinnamon
  sugar

- Combine the #1 ingredients in a blender, blend until smooth, and serve.

Goes well with *Sweet Corn Bread with a Surprise*, page 189.

Chocolate Cream Dessert Soup

about 4 16-ounce servings

#1 Ingredient
1 cup uncooked small, shaped
  pasta

Topper/marshmallow cream
  sauce (in the jar)

#2 Ingredients
3 cup half-and-half
1/2 cup fudge sauce
1 16-ounce can pears, diced with
  liquid

- Cook the #1 ingredient, cool off with cold tap water, and drain.
- Mix the #2 ingredients until well blended. Add the #1 ingredient, give a good stir, and serve.

Goes well with *Banana Strawberry Bread*, page 154.

Cold Strawberry Cream Soup

about 4 16-ounce servings

#1 Ingredient
2 10-ounce packages frozen
  strawberries, in syrup,
  defrosted, with liquid

#2 Ingredients
2 pints half-and-half
2 cups strawberry ice cream

Topper/whipped cream with
  grated chocolate

- Combine the #2 ingredients together in a blender, and blend until smooth. Swirl in the #1 ingredient and serve.

Goes well with *Date Nut Bread*, page 147.

Cold Musk Melon Soup

about 4 16-ounce servings

#1 Ingredients
4 cups orange juice
4 cups ripe cantaloupe, seeded
   and diced
¼ cup sugar or to taste

Topper/scoop of vanilla ice cream

• Using a blender, blend the #1 ingredients until smooth, and serve.

Goes well with *Banana Orange Nut Loaf*, page 152.

Gotta-Love-Prunes Soup

about 6 16-ounce servings

#1 Ingredients
1 pint half-and-half
2 cups sour cream
2 16-ounce cans pitted prunes,
   with liquid
1 tablespoon sugar

Topper/your choice

• Combine the #1 ingredients in a blender, blend until smooth, and serve.

Goes well with *Orange Scones*, page 191.

Chapter 12

SOUPS FOR KIDS

ABC'S Chicken and Pasta Soup
about 5 16-ounce servings

#1 Ingredients
6 cups chicken stock
2 cups chicken, cut into kid-sized
    bites
1 cup celery, diced small
1/2 cup onion, diced small
    (optional)
1/2 cup carrots, grated
salt and pepper to taste

#2 Ingredient
1/2 cup uncooked ABC pasta or
    other fun pasta

Topper/corn chips

- Combine the #1 ingredients in a large soup pot and bring to a simmer for 10 minutes. Add the #2 ingredient and continue to simmer until the pasta is cooked. Serve.

Goes well with *Peanut Butter Bread*, page 150.

ABC Meatball Soup for Kids
about 6 8-ounce servings

#1 Ingredients
1/2 pound hamburger
1/8 teaspoon onion powder
    (optional)

#2 Ingredients
4 cups beef stock
1 cup celery, sliced thin
1/2 cup carrots, grated

1/2 cup the kid's favorite fresh
    veggie, canned or frozen
1/2 cup uncooked ABC pasta for
    soups
salt and pepper to taste

Topper/popcorn

- Mix and form the #1 ingredients into kid-sized meatballs, brown and drain.
- Combine the #1 and #2 ingredients in a large soup pot and bring to a simmer for 20 minutes.

Goes well with *Banana Bread with Almonds*, page 152.

Macaroni and Cheese Soup

about 6 16-ounce servings

#1 Ingredients
4 cups chicken stock
1/2 cup onion, finely diced
1/2 cup carrots, grated
1 cup celery, finely diced

#2 Ingredient
1 cup uncooked kid's favorite pasta

#3 Ingredients
1 cup half-and-half
1 cup sour cream
2 cups American cheese, finely
   diced

Topper/animal crackers

- Mix the #3 ingredients, and set aside.
- Cook, rinse, and drain the #2 ingredient. Set aside.
- Combine the #1 ingredients in a large soup pot and bring to a simmer for 20 minutes. Slowly add the #3 ingredients, stirring constantly until the cheese is melted. Fold in the #2 ingredient and serve.

Goes well with *Banana Scones*, page 191.

Variation: You can add 2 cups of smoked ham to the #1 ingredients for something different.

Spaghetti Soup

about 5 16-ounce servings

#1 Ingredients
6 slices bacon, diced
1 pound lean ground beef
1/2 pound mild pork sausage,
   ground
1/2 cup onion, finely diced

#2 Ingredients
2 14-ounce cans stewed tomatoes
4 cups beef stock
1 cup frozen peas

#3 Ingredient
2 cups spaghetti, broken into
   1-inch pieces

Topper/American cheese,
   shredded

- Cook and drain the #3 ingredient and set aside.
- Brown and drain the #1 ingredients. Combine the #1 and #2 ingredients in a large soup pot. Bring to a simmer for 20 minutes. Add the #3 ingredient, let heat through, and serve.

Goes well with *Tall Biscuits*, page 168.

Chili and Macaroni

about 4 16-ounce servings

#1 Ingredients
1 pound hamburger
1/2 cup onion, chopped

#2 Ingredient
1 1-ounce envelope chili mix

#3 Ingredients
2 cups beef stock ˙
2 14-ounce cans stewed tomatoes
1 15-ounce can kidney beans,
   drained
salt and pepper to taste

#4 Ingredient
1 cup uncooked elbow macaroni

Topper/crushed chili cheese
Fritos

• Cook and drain the #4 ingredient, set aside.
• Brown and drain the #1 ingredients. Return to the heat and mix in the #2 ingredient. (Do not follow the chili seasoning package directions).
• Combine the #1, #2, and #3 ingredients together in a large soup pot and bring to a simmer for 30 minutes. Add the #4 ingredients, stir, and serve.

Goes well with *Frito Corn Bread*, page 187.

Franks and Beans Soup

about 5 8-ounce servings

#1 Ingredients
2 cups chicken stock
1/2 package (4) hot dogs, diced
1 15-ounce can baked beans
1/4 cup brown sugar
3 tablespoons catsup

1/2 tablespoon mustard (optional)
2 tablespoons green onions, sliced
   thin (optional)
3 tablespoons maple syrup

Topper/corn chips

• Combine the #1 ingredients in a large soup pot, bring to a simmer for 30 minutes, and serve.

Goes well with *Basic Bread Sticks*, page 198.

Cold Peanut and Banana Soup

TRY IT, YOU'LL LOVE IT!

about 3 16-ounce servings

#1 Ingredients
1 pint half-and-half
4 ripe bananas, sliced
2 cups milk
1 cup vanilla ice cream
salt to taste

Topper/whipped cream with
chopped peanuts

• Using a blender, blend the #1 ingredient until smooth and serve.

Goes well with *Peanutty Banana Bread*, page 153.

Pumpkin Pie Soup

about 4 16-ounce servings

#1 Ingredients
4 cups apple juice
1 pint heavy cream
1 16-ounce can pumpkin
1/2 teaspoon allspice
1/2 cup sugar

Topper/whipped cream with a
sprinkle of nutmeg

• Using a blender, blend the #1 ingredients until smooth and serve.

Goes well with *Banana Bread with Almonds*, page 152.

Kid's Peppermint Stick Soup

about 4 16-ounce servings

#1 Ingredients
2 cups milk
2 pints half-and-half
4 cups peppermint ice cream

#2 Ingredient
chocolate fudge (in a squirt bottle)

Topper/whipped cream with
grated chocolate and crushed
peppermint stick candy

• Combine the #1 ingredients in a blender, blend until smooth and serve.
Make a swirl in each serving with the #2 ingredient.

Goes well with *Butterscotch Tea Bread*, page 157.

Orange Cream Sickle Soup

#1 Ingredients
1 pint half-and-half
2 cups milk
1 12-ounce can frozen orange
    juice concentrate

1 tablespoon sugar
2 cups vanilla ice cream

Topper/whipped cream with
    sliced oranges

• Using a blender, blend the #1 ingredients together until smooth and serve.

Goes well with *Grape Nut Quickbread*, page 156.

The Best Ever Fruit Soup

about 6 16-ounce servings

#1 Ingredients
1 16-ounce can crushed
    pineapple, with liquid
1 11-ounce can mandarin orange
    slices, with liquid

#2 Ingredients
1 3.4-ounce box instant lemon
    pudding
1 pint half-and-half

#3 Ingredients
1/2 cup fresh strawberries, sliced
1/2 cup fresh blueberries
1/2 cup banana, sliced

Topper/whipped cream

• Using two bowls, separate the #1 ingredients, putting the liquids in one bowl and the fruit in the other.
• Mix the liquids from the #1 ingredients with the #2 ingredients using a wire whisk. Fold the #1,#2, and #3 ingredients together, blending well. Serve.

Goes well with *Banana Strawberry Bread*, page 154.

Chapter 13

SAVORY LOAF BREADS

When mixing quickbreads, be careful not to overmix. Stir until just blended.

Italian Loaf

Preheat oven to 400°

MAKES 1 LOAF

#1 Ingredients
2 cups all-purpose flour
3 teaspoons baking powder
1 teaspoon salt
1 tablespoon Italian seasoning
1 tablespoon dried onion flakes
2 tablespoon fresh parsley,
    chopped (tops only)

#2 Ingredients
1/4 cup melted butter or margarine
1 cup milk
2 eggs, beaten

- Mix the #1 ingredients together with a wire whisk. Mix the #2 ingredients together with a wire whisk.
- Mix the #1 and #2 ingredients together with a wooden spoon.
- Pour into a 9 x 5 greased loaf pan and bake for 50 to 60 minutes, or until an inserted toothpick comes out clean.

Quickbread with Dill

Preheat oven to 400°

MAKES 1 LOAF

#1 Ingredients
2 cups all-purpose flour
2 teaspoons baking powder
1 teaspoon sugar
2 tablespoons dry dill weed
2 tablespoons dry onion flakes

#2 Ingredients
1 cup milk
3 tablespoons olive oil
2 eggs, beaten

- Mix the #1 ingredients together with a wire whisk. Mix the #2 ingredients together with a wire whisk.
- Mix the #1 and #2 ingredients together with a wooden spoon.
- Pour into a greased 9 x 5 loaf pan and bake for 35 to 40 minutes, or until an inserted toothpick comes out clean.

Southwest Loaf

Preheat oven to 400°

MAKES 1 LOAF

#1 Ingredients
2 cups all-purpose flour
3 teaspoons baking powder
1 teaspoon salt
2 tablespoons Parmesan cheese
2 tablespoons onion, minced
1 tablespoons fresh basil, chopped
1/4 teaspoon garlic powder
1/4 teaspoon crushed red pepper,
  or to taste

#2 Ingredients
1/4 cup melted butter or margarine
3/4 cup milk
1 egg, beaten

- Mix the #1 ingredients together with a wire whisk. Mix #2 ingredients together with a wire whisk.
- Mix the #1 and #2 ingredients together with a wooden spoon. The dough should be lumpy.
- Pour into a 9 x 5 greased loaf pan and bake for 60 minutes, or until an inserted toothpick comes out clean.

Anise Seed Bread

Preheat oven to 400°

MAKES 1 LOAF

#1 Ingredients
2 cups all-purpose flour
3 teaspoons baking powder
1 teaspoon salt
2 tablespoons anise seeds

#2 Ingredients
1/4 cup melted butter or margarine
3/4 cup milk
2 eggs, beaten

Topper/pat of butter and small
  red bell pepper, diced

- Mix #1 ingredients together with a wire whisk. Mix #2 ingredients together with a wire whisk.
- Mix the #1 and #2 ingredients together with a wooden spoon. The dough should be fairly thin.
- Pour into a 9 x 5 greased loaf pan and bake for 50 to 60 minutes, or until an inserted toothpick comes out clean.

Quick Curry Bread

Preheat oven to 400°

MAKES 1 LOAF

#1 Ingredients
2 cups all-purpose flour
3 teaspoons baking powder
1 teaspoon salt
1/2 teaspoon baking soda

#2 Ingredients
3 tablespoons sugar
1/4 cup milk
1/4 cup melted butter or margarine
3 eggs, beaten
1 cup sour cream
1/2 tablespoon curry powder
1 tablespoon dried onion flakes

- Mix the #1 ingredients together with a wire whisk. Mix the #2 ingredients together with a wire whisk.
- Mix the #1 and #2 ingredients together with a wooden spoon until just blended.
- Pour into a greased 9 X 5 loaf pan and bake for 55 to 60 minutes, or until an inserted toothpick comes out clean.

Garlic Loaf

Preheat oven to 375°

MAKES 1 LOAF

#1 Ingredients
2 cups all-purpose flour
3 teaspoons baking powder
1 tablespoon sugar
1 teaspoon salt

#2 Ingredients
3 tablespoons garlic, minced, or to taste
1 egg, beaten
1 cup milk
2 tablespoons melted butter

- Mix the #1 ingredients together with a wire whisk. Mix the #2 ingredients together with a wire whisk.
- Mix the #1 and the #2 ingredients together using a wooden spoon.
- Pour into a greased 9 x 5 loaf pan and bake 45 to 50 minutes, or until an inserted toothpick comes out clean.

Sunflower Seed Bread

Preheat oven to 400°

MAKES 1 LOAF

#1 Ingredients
2 cups all-purpose flour
3 teaspoons baking powder
1 teaspoon salt
1/3 cup sunflower seeds, chopped

#2 Ingredients
1/4 cup melted butter or margarine
1 cup milk
2 eggs, beaten

- Mix the #1 ingredients together with a fork. Mix the #2 ingredients together with a wire whisk.
- Mix the #1 and #2 ingredients together with a wooden spoon. The batter should be lumpy.
- Pour into a 9 X 5 greased loaf pan and bake for 55 to 60 minutes, or until an inserted toothpick comes out clean.

Veggie Bread

Preheat oven to 400°

MAKES 1 LOAF

#1 Ingredients
3 cups all-purpose flour
3 1/2 teaspoons baking powder
1 teaspoon salt
1 tablespoon each, diced very
  small: yellow bell pepper, green
  bell pepper, red bell pepper,
  and onion
1 tablespoon each: carrot and
  zucchini, diced small
1 tablespoon celery leaves,
  chopped

#2 Ingredients
1/4 cup melted butter or margarine
3/4 cup milk
2 eggs, beaten

- Mix #1 ingredients together with a fork. Mix #2 ingredients together with a wire whisk.
- Mix the #1 and #2 ingredients together with a wooden spoon. The dough should be lumpy.
- Pour into a 9 x 5 greased loaf pan and bake for 60 minutes, or until an inserted toothpick comes out clean.

Black Bread

Preheat oven to 375°

MAKES 1 LOAF

#1 Ingredients
2 cups all-purpose flour
3 teaspoons baking powder
1 teaspoon salt
1/2 teaspoon baking soda
3 tablespoons instant coffee
2 tablespoons dried onion flakes

#2 Ingredients
1/4 cup melted butter or margarine
1 cup milk
2 eggs, beaten
1/4 cup dark molasses

- Mix #1 ingredients together with a wire whisk. Mix #2 ingredients together with a wire whisk.
- Mix the #1 and #2 ingredients together with a wooden spoon. The dough should be thick.
- Pour into a 9 x 5 greased loaf pan and bake for 55 to 60 minutes, or until an inserted toothpick comes out clean.

Celery-Poppy Seed-Onion Bread

Preheat oven to 400°

MAKES 1 LOAF

#1 Ingredients
2 cups all-purpose flour
3 teaspoons baking powder
1 teaspoon salt
1/4 cup celery, diced small
1/4 cup onion, diced small
1 tablespoon celery leaves,
    chopped
2 tablespoons poppy seeds

#2 Ingredients
1/4 cup melted butter or margarine
1/2 cup milk
1 10 1/2-ounce can cream of celery
    soup
2 eggs, beaten

- Mix #1 ingredients together with a fork. Mix #2 ingredients together with a wire whisk.
- Mix the #1 and #2 ingredients together with a wooden spoon. The dough should be thick and lumpy.
- Pour into a 9 x 5 greased loaf pan and bake 60 minutes, or until an inserted toothpick comes out clean.

A Dill Zucchini Loaf

Preheat oven to 350°

MAKES 1 LOAF

#1 Ingredients
2 cups all-purpose flour
1 teaspoon salt
3 teaspoons baking powder
2 tablespoons dill weed

#2 Ingredients
1 egg, beaten
2 tablespoons oil
1 cup milk
1 cup grated zucchini (drained on
a paper towel)

- Mix the #1 ingredients together with a wire whisk. Mix the #2 ingredients together with a wire whisk.
- Mix the #1 and the #2 ingredients together with a wooden spoon and pour into a greased 8 x 4 loaf pan.
- Bake 45 to 50 minutes, or until an inserted toothpick comes out clean.

Onion Sage Bread

Preheat oven to 375°

MAKES 1 LOAF

#1 Ingredients
2 cups all-purpose flour
3 teaspoons baking powder
1 teaspoon salt
1 cup onion, chopped very small
3 teaspoons fresh sage, finely
chopped, or 1½ teaspoons
dry sage leaves

#2 Ingredients
1 cup milk
¼ cup melted butter or margarine
1 egg, beaten

- Mix the #1 ingredients together with a fork. Mix the #2 ingredients together with a wire whisk.
- Mix the #1 and #2 ingredients together with a wooden spoon. The batter should be thick and lumpy.
- Pour into a greased 9 x 5 loaf pan and bake for 60 minutes, or until an inserted toothpick comes out clean.

Pickle in a Loaf

Preheat oven to 400°

MAKES 1 LOAF

#1 Ingredients
2 cups all-purpose flour
3 teaspoons baking powder
1 teaspoon salt
1/2 teaspoon baking soda
1/2 cup dill pickle relish

#2 Ingredients
1/4 cup melted butter or margarine
3/4 cup milk
1 egg, beaten
1/4 cup pickle juice

- Mix the #1 ingredients together with a wire whisk. Mix the #2 ingredients together with a wire whisk.
- Mix the #1 and #2 ingredients together with a wooden spoon until blended.
- Pour into a greased 9 x 5 loaf pan and bake for 55 to 60 minutes or until an inserted toothpick comes out clean.

Herb and Onion Loaf

Preheat oven to 425°

MAKES 1 LOAF

#1 Ingredients
2 cups all-purpose flour
3 teaspoons baking powder
1 teaspoon salt
1/4 teaspoon baking soda
2 1/2 tablespoons fresh parsley, chopped (tops only)
1 tablespoon fresh cilantro, chopped
1 tablespoon fresh oregano, chopped
1/2 teaspoon garlic powder
1/2 cup onion, diced very small

#2 Ingredients
1/4 cup melted butter
3/4 cup milk
1 egg, beaten

- Mix the #1 ingredients together with a fork. Mix the #2 ingredients together with a wire whisk.
- Mix the #1 and #2 ingredients together with a wooden spoon. The dough should be lumpy but well mixed.
- Pour into a greased 9 x 5 loaf pan and bake for 55 to 60 minutes, or until an inserted toothpick comes out clean.

Sour Cream and Onion Loaf

Preheat oven to 400°

MAKES 1 LOAF

#1 Ingredients
3 cups all-purpose flour
3½ teaspoons baking powder
1 teaspoon salt
½ teaspoon baking soda
½ cup sour cream and onion
   potato chips, crushed

#2 Ingredients
2 tablespoons oil
1 cup milk
2 eggs, beaten
1 cup sour cream

- Mix #1 ingredients together with a wire whisk. Mix #2 ingredients together with a wire whisk.
- Mix the #1 and #2 ingredients together with a wooden spoon. The dough should be on the thin side.
- Pour into a 9 x 5 greased loaf pan and bake for 50 to 60 minutes, or until an inserted toothpick comes out clean.

Confetti Casserole Bread

Preheat oven to 400°

MAKES 1 LOAF

#1 Ingredients
2 cups all-purpose flour
3 teaspoons baking powder
1 teaspoon salt
½ teaspoon baking soda
¼ cup onion, finely chopped
2 teaspoons dry mustard
1 1-ounce envelope dried
   vegetable soup mix
½ cup crushed corned chips

#2 Ingredients
1 tablespoon tomato paste
¼ cup butter, softened
¼ cup soft cream cheese
1⅔ cup milk
2 eggs, beaten

- Mix the #1 ingredients together with a wire whisk. Mix the #2 ingredients together with an electric mixer until smooth.
- Mix the #1 and #2 ingredients together with a wooden spoon.
- Pour into a well greased, oven proof 2-quart bowl, and bake 55 to 60 minutes, or until an inserted toothpick comes out clean.

3-Bean Sprout Bread

Preheat oven to 400°

MAKES 1 LOAF

#1 Ingredients
2 cups all-purpose flour
3 teaspoons baking powder
1 teaspoon salt
1/2 cup soybean sprouts, chopped
1/2 cup alfalfa sprouts, chopped
1/2 cup mung bean sprouts,
    chopped

#2 Ingredients
1/4 cup melted butter or margarine
1 cup milk
1 egg, beaten

- Mix #1 ingredients together with a fork. Mix #2 ingredients together with a wire whisk.
- Mix the #1 and #2 ingredients together with a wooden spoon. The dough should be thick and lumpy.
- Pour into a 9 x 5 greased loaf pan and bake for 60 minutes, or until an inserted toothpick comes out clean.

Buttery Beer Bread

Preheat oven to 375°

MAKES 1 LOAF

#1 Ingredients
3 cups all-purpose flour
1 12-ounce can of your favorite
    beer
1 teaspoon salt

#2 Ingredient
1 stick butter, melted and divided
    in half

- Mix the #1 ingredients together (don't mix until smooth. The batter should be lumpy).
- Pour half the #2 ingredient into a 8 x 4 loaf pan, coating all sides. The butter will pool in the bottom of the pan.
- Pour the #1 ingredients into the loaf pan and pour the remaining #2 ingredients over the batter.
- Bake 50 to 60 minutes or until an inserted toothpick comes out clean.

Variation: Add 1 tablespoon Italian seasoning, and 1 1/2 cups mozzarella cheese to the #1 ingredients for a cheesy herb beer bread.

Scottish Buttermilk Bread

Preheat oven to 375°

MAKES 1 LOAF

#1 Ingredients
2 cups all-purpose flour
3 teaspoons baking powder
1 teaspoon salt
1/2 teaspoon baking soda
1 tablespoon sugar
1/8 teaspoon cream of tarter

#2 Ingredients
1 cup buttermilk
1/4 cup melted butter or margarine

#3 Ingredient
3 tablespoons melted butter

- Mix the #1 ingredients together with a wire whisk. Mix the #2 ingredients together with a wire whisk.
- Mix the #1 and #2 ingredients together with a wooden spoon, just until blended.
- Pour into a greased 9 X 5 loaf pan and pour the #3 ingredients over the top.
- Bake for 50 to 60 minutes, or until an inserted toothpick comes out clean.

Basic Buttermilk Bread

TO USE OTHER INGREDIENTS, SEE **VARIATIONS** ON PAGE 136.

Preheat oven to 400°

MAKES 1 LOAF

#1 Ingredients
2 cups all-purpose flour
3 teaspoons baking powder
1 teaspoon salt
1/2 teaspoon baking soda

#2 Ingredients
1 cup buttermilk
1/4 cup melted butter or margarine
1 egg, beaten

- Mix the #1 ingredients together with a wire whisk. Mix the #2 ingredients together with a wire whisk.
- Mix the #1 and #2 ingredients together with a wooden spoon just until blended.
- Pour into a greased 9 x 5 loaf pan and bake 50 to 60 minutes, or until an inserted tooth pick comes out clean.

Cream Cheese and Chives Loaf

Preheat oven to 400°

MAKES 1 LOAF

#1 Ingredients
2 cups all-purpose flour
3 teaspoons baking powder
1 teaspoon salt
1/2 teaspoon baking soda
4 tablespoons dried chives

#2 Ingredients
1 cup soft cream cheese
1/3 cup melted butter or margarine
1 cup milk
1 egg, beaten

- Mix #1 ingredients together with a wire whisk. Mix #2 ingredients together with an electric mixer until smooth.
- Mix the #1 and #2 ingredients together with a wooden spoon.
- Pour into a 9 x 5 greased loaf pan and bake 60 minutes, or until an inserted toothpick comes out clean.

Olive and Cream Cheese Loaf

Preheat oven to 400°

MAKES 1 LOAF

#1 Ingredients
2 cups all-purpose flour
3 teaspoons baking powder
1 teaspoon salt
1/2 teaspoon baking soda
2/3 cup green salad olives,
    chopped and drained

#2 Ingredients
1/4 cup melted butter or margarine
1 cup milk
1 egg, beaten

- Mix #1 ingredients together with a fork. Mix #2 ingredients together with a wire whisk.
- Mix the #1 and #2 ingredients together with a wooden spoon. The dough should be lumpy.
- Pour into a 9 x 5 greased loaf pan and bake 55 to 60 minutes, or until an inserted toothpick comes out clean.

Variations:
Just follow the Basic Buttermilk Bread recipe on page 134.
Try combining some of the different ingredients.

INGREDIENTS	AMOUNT	SPECIAL DIRECTIONS
Celery and Onion	1 teaspoon celery seed, 1 teaspoon paprika, 1/2 cup celery, sliced thin, 1/4 cup onion, diced small	Mix with the #1 ingredients
Cheese: Colby, cheddar, mozzarella, American cheese, etc	2 cups your choice, shredded 2/3 cup Parmesan	Mix with the #1 ingredients
Dried Fruits and Nuts	1 cup dried fruit, diced very small, and 1/2 to 2/3 cup sugar	Mix with the #1 ingredients. If using both dried fruits and nuts, use 1/2 cup of each
Green Onion and Poppy	3 tablespoons poppy seeds and 2/3 cup green onion, sliced thin	Mix with the #1 ingredients
Herbs (fresh)	3 tablespoons of the following: tarragon, oregano, basil, marjoram, sage, cilantro, and parsley, chopped	Mix with the #1 ingredients
Meat: ham, chicken, sausage, etc. (cooked)	1 cup, diced small	Mix with the #1 ingredients
Onion and Dill	2/3 cup onion, diced small, 3 tablespoons dill weed, and 1/4 cup onion powder	Mix with the #1 ingredients
Onion Soup Mix	1 cup cheddar cheese, shredded and 1 1-ounce envelope onion soup mix	Mix with the #1 ingredients
Sesame Seed	1 1/2 tablespoons toasted sesame seeds and 1 tablespoon sesame seed oil	Mix the seeds with the #1 ingredients Mix the oil with the #2 ingredients
Veggies: broccoli, spinach, cooked and drained	2 cups, chopped small	Mix with the #1 ingredients

Philly Poppy Seed Loaf

Preheat oven to 375°

MAKES 1 LOAF

#1 Ingredients
2 cups all-purpose flour
3 teaspoons baking powder
1 teaspoon salt
1/2 teaspoon baking soda
2/3 cup onion, diced very small
2 tablespoons poppy seeds

#2 Ingredients
1 cup milk
1/4 cup melted butter or margarine
1 egg, beaten

#3 Ingredients
1 8-ounce tub of soft cream
  cheese
2 eggs, beaten
1 teaspoon poppy seeds
1/2 cup onion, finely diced
2 tablespoons milk
1/8 teaspoon salt

- Mix the #3 ingredients together with an electric mixer until well blended and set aside.
- Mix the #1 ingredients together with a wire whisk. Mix the #2 ingredients together with a wire whisk.
- Mix the #1 and #2 ingredients together with a wooden spoon just until blended.
- Pour into a greased 9 x 5 loaf pan, pour the #3 ingredients over the top and bake for 55 to 60 minutes, or until an inserted toothpick comes out clean.

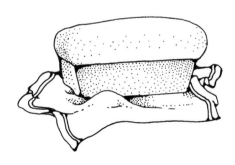

Sharp Cheddar Quickbread

Preheat oven to 400°

MAKES 1 LOAF

#1 Ingredients
2 cups all-purpose flour
3 teaspoons baking powder
1 teaspoon salt

#2 Ingredients
1 cup milk
1/4 cup melted butter or margarine
1 egg, beaten
2 cups sharp cheddar cheese, shredded

- Mix the #1 ingredients together with a wire whisk. Mix the #2 ingredients together with a fork.
- Mix the #1 and #2 ingredients together with a wooden spoon just until blended.
- Pour into a greased 9 x 5 loaf pan and bake 60 minutes, or until an inserted toothpick comes out clean.

Swiss Cheese Bread with Mustard

Preheat oven to 375°

MAKES 1 LOAF

#1 Ingredients
2 cups all-purpose flour
3 teaspoons baking powder
1 teaspoon salt
2 teaspoons dry mustard

#2 Ingredients
1 cup milk
1/4 cup melted butter or margarine
2 eggs, beaten
2 cups Swiss cheese, shredded

- Mix the #1 ingredients together with a wire whisk. Mix the #2 ingredients together with a fork.
- Mix the #1 and #2 ingredients together with a wooden spoon. The batter should be lumpy.
- Pour into a greased 9 x 5 loaf pan and bake 55 to 60 minutes, or until an inserted toothpick comes out clean.

Cheesy Ham Bread

Preheat oven to 350°

MAKES 1 LOAF

#1 Ingredients
2 cups all-purpose flour
3 teaspoons baking powder
1 teaspoon salt
1 cup smoked ham, diced small
1/2 cup Monterey Jack cheese,
    shredded
1/2 cup Swiss cheese, shredded

#2 Ingredients
2 eggs, beaten
1 cup milk

- Mix the #1 ingredients together with a fork. Mix the #2 ingredients together with a wire whisk.
- Mix the #1 and the #2 ingredients together with a wooden spoon.
- Pour into a well greased 9 x 5 loaf pan and bake for 55 to 60 minutes or until an inserted toothpick comes out clean.

Poppy Seed, Cheese, and Chive Bread

Preheat oven to 400°

MAKES 1 LOAF

#1 Ingredients
2 cups all-purpose flour
3 teaspoons baking powder
1 teaspoon salt
4 tablespoons poppy seeds
2/3 cup fresh chives, sliced thin

#2 Ingredients
1 cup milk
1/4 cup melted butter or margarine
2 eggs, beaten
2 cups Colby cheese, shredded

- Mix the #1 ingredients together with a wire whisk. Mix the #2 ingredients together with a fork.
- Mix the #1 and #2 ingredients together with a wooden spoon just until blended.
- Pour into a greased 9 x 5 loaf pan and bake 60 minutes, or until an inserted toothpick comes out clean.

Salsa Loaf

ONE OF OUR SUNDAY MORNING FAVORITES:
GOES WELL WITH SOFT CREAM CHEESE.

Preheat oven to 400°

MAKES 1 LOAF

#1 Ingredients
2 cups all-purpose flour
3 teaspoons baking powder
1/2 teaspoon salt
1/2 teaspoon baking soda
2 cups mozzarella cheese,
　shredded

#2 Ingredients
2 cups salsa (homemade or extra
　chunky)
1 tablespoon milk
1 egg, beaten

- Mix the #1 ingredients together with a wire whisk. Mix the #2 ingredients together with a wire whisk.
- Mix the #1 and the #2 ingredients together with a wooden spoon. The dough should be lumpy and thick, but you should still be able to pour it.
- Pour into a 9 x 5 greased loaf pan and bake for 40 to 45 minutes, or until an inserted toothpick comes out clean.

Broccoli and Onion Bread with Cheese

Preheat oven to 400°

MAKES 1 LOAF

#1 Ingredients
2 cups all-purpose flour
3 teaspoons baking powder
1 teaspoon salt
1 cup fresh broccoli florets,
　chopped small and cooked until
　tender and drained, or 1 10-
　ounce package frozen,
　chopped broccoli, defrosted
　and drained
1/2 cup red onion, diced very small

#2 Ingredients
1/4 cup melted butter or margarine
1 cup milk
1 egg, beaten
2 cups sharp cheddar cheese,
　shredded

- Mix the #1 ingredients together with a fork. Mix the #2 ingredients together with a fork.
- Mix the #1 and #2 ingredients together with a wooden spoon. The batter should be thick.
- Pour into a 9 x 5 greased loaf pan and bake 60 minutes, or until an inserted toothpick comes out clean.

Spinach Loaf with Cheese

Preheat oven to 375°

MAKES 1 LOAF

#1 Ingredients
2 cups all-purpose flour
3 teaspoons baking powder
2 tablespoons dried onion flakes
2 cups sharp cheddar cheese,
    shredded

#2 Ingredients
1 cup milk
1 egg, beaten
1 cup fresh spinach, chopped and
    packed, or 1/2 cup frozen
    chopped spinach, defrosted,
    with the moisture squeezed out
2 tablespoons olive oil

- Mix the #1 ingredients together with a wire whisk. Mix the #2 ingredients together with a wire whisk.
- Mix the #1 and #2 ingredients together using a wooden spoon.
- Pour into a greased 9 x 5 loaf pan and bake 50 to 60 minutes, or until an inserted toothpick comes out clean.

Potato Onion Bread with Cheese

Preheat oven to 400°

MAKES 1 LOAF

#1 Ingredients
2 cups all-purpose flour
3 teaspoons baking powder
1 teaspoon salt
1/2 cup green onions, sliced thin

2 eggs, beaten
1 cup mashed potatoes (can be
    instant, just follow package
    directions)
2 cups mozzarella cheese,
    shredded

#2 Ingredients
1/4 cup melted butter or margarine
1 cup milk

#3 Ingredient
1 stick melted butter, divided in half

- Mix the #1 ingredients together with a fork. Mix the #2 ingredients together with a wire whisk.
- Mix the #1 and #2 ingredients together with a wooden spoon.
- Pour half the #3 ingredients into a 9 x 5 loaf pan, coating all sides of the pan.
- Pour the batter into the same loaf pan. Pour the remaining #3 ingredients over the top of the batter and bake 55 to 60 minutes, or until an inserted toothpick comes out clean.

Parmesan Garlic Loaf

Preheat oven to 400°

MAKES 1 LOAF

#1 Ingredients
2 cups all-purpose flour
3 teaspoons baking powder
1 teaspoon salt
2/3 cups Parmesan cheese

#2 Ingredients
1/4 cup melted butter or margarine
1 cup milk
2 eggs, beaten
1 tablespoon garlic, minced

#3 Ingredient
3 tablespoons Parmesan cheese

- Mix the #1 ingredients together with a wire whisk. Mix the #2 ingredients together with a wire whisk.
- Mix the #1 and #2 ingredients together with a wooden spoon. The batter should be lumpy.
- Pour into a 9 x 5 greased loaf pan and sprinkle the #3 ingredient over the top.
- Bake for 55 to 60 minutes or until an inserted toothpick comes out clean.

Mustardy Cheese Bread

Preheat oven to 350°

MAKES 1 LOAF

#1 Ingredients
2 cups all-purpose flour
3 teaspoons baking powder
1 teaspoon salt
2 cups mozzarella cheese,
    shredded

#2 Ingredients
3/4 cup milk
1 tablespoon spicy mustard
1/4 cup butter, melted
2 eggs, beaten

- Mix the #1 ingredients together with a fork. Mix the #2 ingredients together with a wire whisk.
- Mix the #1 and the #2 ingredients together using a wooden spoon.
- Pour into a 9 x 5 greased loaf pan and bake 50 to 60 minutes, or until an inserted toothpick comes out clean.

Wine and Cheese Bread

Preheat oven to 375°

MAKES 1 LOAF

#1 Ingredients
2 cups all-purpose flour
3 teaspoons baking powder
1 teaspoon salt
1/2 teaspoon baking soda
1/4 teaspoon cream of tarter
1 teaspoon dried oregano
1 tablespoon dried onion flakes

#2 Ingredients
1 cup milk
1/4 cup melted butter or margarine
1 egg, beaten
1/2 cup port wine
2 cups sharp cheddar cheese,
  shredded

- Mix the #1 ingredients together with a wire whisk. Mix the #2 ingredients together with a fork.
- Mix the #1 and #2 ingredients together with a wooden spoon.
- Pour into a greased 9 x 5 loaf pan and bake 60 minutes, or until an inserted toothpick comes out clean.

Three Cheese Wine Bread

Preheat oven to 400°

MAKES 1 LOAF

#1 Ingredients
2 cups all-purpose flour
3 teaspoons baking powder
1 tablespoon sugar
1 tablespoon dry onion flakes
1/8 teaspoon oregano
1 tablespoon fresh basil, chopped
1/2 teaspoon fresh parsley,
  chopped
1 teaspoon salt

1/2 cup Parmesan cheese, grated
1/2 cup mozzarella cheese,
  shredded
1 cup sharp cheddar cheese,
  shredded

#2 Ingredients
1/4 cup melted butter
1 cup dry red wine
1 egg, beaten

- Mix the #1 ingredients together with a fork. Mix the #2 ingredients together with a wire whisk.
- Mix the #1 and #2 ingredients together with a wooden spoon.
- Pour into a greased 8 x 5 loaf pan and bake for 50 to 60 minutes, or until an inserted toothpick comes out clean.

Cheese Beer Bread with a Kick

Preheat oven to 400°

MAKES 1 LOAF

#1 Ingredients
3 cups all-purpose flour
3 teaspoons baking powder
1 teaspoon salt
1/2 teaspoon baking soda
1 3-ounce can chopped green
    chiles, drained

#2 Ingredients
1 12-ounce can of your favorite
    beer
2 cups jalapeño cheese, shredded

- Mix the #1 ingredients together with a fork. Mix the #2 ingredients together with a fork.
- Mix the #1 and #2 ingredients together with a wooden spoon.
- Pour into a greased 9 x 5 loaf pan and bake 60 minutes, or until an inserted toothpick comes out clean.

Chapter 14

SWEET LOAF BREADS

Lemony Golden Raisin Bread

Preheat oven to 375°

MAKES 1 LOAF

#1 Ingredients
2 cups all-purpose flour
3 teaspoons baking powder
1 teaspoon salt
2/3 cup sugar
2/3 cup golden raisins
1/2 cup chopped nuts (your choice)
2 tablespoons lemon zest

#2 Ingredients
1/4 cup melted butter or margarine
1 cup milk
2 eggs, beaten
1 teaspoon lemon extract
3 tablespoons fresh lemon juice

#3 Ingredient
2 tablespoons fresh lemon juice

#4 Ingredient
2 tablespoons sugar

- Mix the #1 ingredients together with a fork. Mix the #2 ingredients together with a wire whisk.
- Mix the #1 and #2 ingredients together with a wooden spoon, until just blended.
- Pour into a greased 9 x 5 loaf pan. Pour the #3 ingredient over the top.
- Sprinkle with the #4 ingredient and bake 55 to 60 minutes or until an inserted toothpick comes out clean.

Variation: Reduce the golden raisins to 1/2 cup or omit. Add 1 cup Granny Smith apples, peeled and diced small, to the #1 ingredients.

Lemon Poppy Bread

Preheat oven to 400°

MAKES 1 LOAF

#1 Ingredients
2 cups all-purpose flour
3 teaspoons baking powder
1 teaspoon salt
1 cup sugar
3 tablespoons poppy seeds

#2 Ingredients
1/4 cup butter
1 cup milk
1 egg, beaten
4 tablespoons fresh lemon juice
1 tablespoon lemon zest
1/2 teaspoon lemon extract

- Mix the #1 ingredients together with a wire whisk. Mix the #2 ingredients together with a wire whisk.
- Mix the #1 and #2 ingredients together with a wooden spoon.
- Pour into a greased 9 x 5 loaf pan and bake 50 to 60 minutes or until an inserted toothpick comes out clean.

Poppy Sesame Tea Bread

Preheat oven to 400°

MAKES 1 LOAF

#1 Ingredients
3 cups all-purpose flour
1 1/2 teaspoons baking powder
1 teaspoon salt
1/2 cup sugar
1/4 cup toasted sesame seeds
1/4 cup poppy seeds

#2 Ingredients
1/4 cup melted butter
1 1/2 cups milk
2 eggs, beaten

- Mix the #1 ingredients together with a wire whisk. Mix the #2 ingredients together with a fork.
- Mix the #1 and #2 ingredients together with a wooden spoon.
- Pour into a greased 9 x 5 inch loaf pan and bake for 55 to 60 minutes or until an inserted toothpick comes out clean.

Orange Spice Bread

Preheat oven to 350°

MAKES 1 LOAF

#1 Ingredients
2 cups all-purpose flour
3 teaspoons baking powder
1 teaspoon salt
1 1/2 tablespoons fresh orange zest
1/4 teaspoon ground allspice
1/4 teaspoon ground cardamom
1/8 teaspoon ground nutmeg

#2 Ingredients
1/4 cup melted butter
1/4 cup honey
1/2 cup milk
2 eggs, beaten
1/4 teaspoon almond extract

- Mix the #1 ingredients together with a wire whisk. Mix the #2 ingredients together with a wire whisk.
- Mix the #1 and #2 ingredients with a wooden spoon.
- Pour into a greased 9 x 5 loaf pan and bake 55 to 60 minutes or until an inserted toothpick comes out clean.

Date Nut Bread

Preheat oven to 400°

MAKES 1 LOAF

#1 Ingredients
2 cups all-purpose flour
3 teaspoons baking powder
1 teaspoon salt
1/2 cup dates, diced small
1 teaspoon ground cinnamon
1/2 cup sugar
1 cup walnuts, chopped

#2 Ingredients
1/4 cup melted butter or margarine
3/4 cup milk
1 egg, beaten

- Mix the #1 ingredients together with a fork. Mix the #2 ingredients together with a wire whisk.
- Mix the #1 and #2 ingredients together with a wooden spoon.
- Pour into a 9 x 5 greased loaf pan and bake 55 minutes or until an inserted toothpick comes out clean.

Fresh Apple Bread

Preheat oven to 375°

MAKES 1 LOAF

#1 Ingredients
2 cups all-purpose flour
1 teaspoon baking powder
1 teaspoon cinnamon
1 teaspoon baking soda
1 cup sugar
1 cup Granny Smith apples, diced
   very small

#2 Ingredients
1 teaspoon vanilla
1/2 cup oil
1/2 cup raisins
1/2 cup nuts, chopped (your
   choice)
1/2 cup milk
1 egg, beaten

- Mix the #1 ingredients together with a wire whisk. Mix the #2 ingredients together with a wire whisk.
- Mix the #1 ingredients and the #2 ingredients together with a wooden spoon.
- Pour into a greased 9 x 5 loaf pan and bake 50 to 60 minutes or until an inserted toothpick comes out clean.

Lemony Almond Bread

Preheat oven to 350°

MAKES 1 LOAF

#1 Ingredients
2 cups all-purpose flour
3 teaspoons baking powder
1/2 cup almonds, sliced and
   toasted
1/2 cup sugar
3 tablespoons fresh lemon zest
1/4 teaspoon salt
1 teaspoon baking soda

#2 Ingredients
2 eggs, beaten
1 tablespoon lemon juice
1/2 teaspoon vanilla extract
1/2 teaspoon almond extract
1/4 cup butter, melted
1 cup buttermilk

- Mix the #1 ingredients together with a wire whisk. Mix the #2 ingredients together with a wire whisk.
- Mix the #1 and #2 ingredients together with a wooden spoon.
- Pour into a greased 9 x 5 loaf pan and bake 50 minutes or until an inserted toothpick comes out clean.

Orange Cranberry Nut Bread

Preheat oven to 400°

MAKES 1 LOAF

#1 Ingredients
2 cups all-purpose flour
3 teaspoons baking powder
1 teaspoon salt
1 cup sugar
1/2 teaspoon baking soda
1 cup walnuts, chopped
1 tablespoon fresh orange zest
1 cup fresh cranberries, chopped
1/2 cup golden raisins
1/4 teaspoon ground nutmeg

#2 Ingredients
1 1/8 cup orange juice
1/4 cup melted butter or margarine
2 eggs, beaten

- Mix the #1 ingredients together with a fork. Mix the #2 ingredients together with a wire whisk.
- Mix the #1 and #2 ingredients together with a wooden spoon.
- Pour into a greased 9 x 5 loaf pan and bake 50 to 60 minutes or until an inserted toothpick comes out clean.

Macadamia Nut Peach Bread

Preheat oven to 375°

MAKES 1 LOAF

#1 Ingredients
2 cups all purpose flour
3 teaspoons baking powder
1/4 teaspoon salt
3 tablespoons sugar
1 cup macadamia nuts, chopped

#2 Ingredients
1 tablespoon melted butter or margarine
1 cup milk
1 cup fresh peaches, diced, or
  1 cup canned peaches, drained and diced
1 egg, beaten

- Mix the #1 ingredients together with a fork. Mix the #2 ingredients together with a fork.
- Mix the #1 and #2 ingredients together with a wooden spoon.
- Pour into a 9 x 5 greased loaf pan and bake for 55 minutes or until an inserted toothpick comes out clean.

Oatmeal Walnut Quickbread

Preheat oven to 400°

MAKES 1 LOAF

#1 Ingredients
2 cups all-purpose flour
3 teaspoons baking powder
1 teaspoon salt
1/2 cup sugar
1 cup quick cooking oatmeal
2/3 cup walnuts, chopped

#2 Ingredients
1/4 cup melted butter or margarine
2 cups milk
1 egg, beaten

#3 Ingredient
2 tablespoons oatmeal

#4 Ingredient
1 egg, beaten

- Mix the #1 ingredients together with a fork. Mix the #2 ingredients together with a wire whisk.
- Mix the #1 and #2 ingredients together with a wooden spoon.
- Pour into a 9 x 5 greased loaf pan and sprinkle the top with the #3 ingredient.
- Brush with the #4 ingredient and bake for 60 minutes or until an inserted toothpick comes out clean.

Peanut Butter Bread

Preheat oven to 350°

MAKES 1 LOAF

#1 Ingredients
2 1/2 cups flour
4 teaspoons baking powder
1 teaspoon salt
1/2 cup sugar

#2 Ingredients
1 1/4 cups milk
2 eggs, beaten
1 cup crunchy or creamy peanut
   butter
2 teaspoons oil

- Mix the #1 ingredients together with a wire whisk. Mix the #2 ingredients together with an electric mixer until smooth.
- Mix the #1 and the #2 ingredients together with a wooden spoon.
- Pour into a greased 9 x 5 loaf pan and bake 50 to 55 minutes or until an inserted toothpick comes out clean.

Variation: Add 1 cup peanuts, chopped small, to the #1 ingredients.

Pumpkin Bread

Preheat oven to 400°

MAKES 1 LOAF

#1 Ingredients
1 cup whole wheat flour
1 cup all-purpose flour
3 teaspoons baking powder
1 teaspoon salt
1/2 cup brown sugar, packed
1/2 teaspoon baking soda
1 teaspoon pumpkin spice
1/2 cup wheat germ
1/2 cup walnuts, chopped

#2 Ingredients
1 1/4 cups buttermilk
1/4 cup melted butter or margarine
3 eggs, beaten
2/3 cup canned pumpkin

- Mix the #1 ingredients together with a fork. Mix the #2 ingredients together with an electric mixer until smooth.
- Mix the #1 and #2 ingredients together with a wooden spoon.
- Pour into a greased 9 x 5 loaf pan and bake 60 minutes or until an inserted toothpick comes out clean.

New England Banana Bread

Preheat oven to 400°

MAKES 1 LOAF

#1 Ingredients
1 1/2 cups all-purpose flour
2 teaspoons baking powder
1/2 teaspoon baking soda
1/2 teaspoon salt
1 cup sugar
1 cup bran cereal
1 cup nuts, chopped (your choice)

#2 Ingredients
1/4 cup melted butter or margarine
2 tablespoons water
2 eggs beaten
1 1/2 cups bananas, mashed

- Mix the #1 ingredients together with a fork. Mix the #2 ingredients together with an electric mixer until smooth.
- Mix the #1 and #2 ingredients together with a wooden spoon.
- Pour into a greased 9 x 5 loaf pan and bake 55 to 60 minutes or until an inserted toothpick comes out clean.

Banana Orange Nut Loaf

Preheat oven to 400°

MAKES 1 LOAF

#1 Ingredients
2 cups all-purpose flour
3 teaspoons baking powder
1 teaspoon salt
2/3 cup sugar
1/2 teaspoon baking soda
1 cup walnuts, chopped small
1 tablespoon fresh orange zest

#2 Ingredients
1 cup fresh orange juice, or 1 cup
    made from concentrate
1/4 cup melted butter or margarine
2 eggs, beaten
1 cup bananas, mashed

- Mix the #1 ingredients together with a fork. Mix the #2 ingredients together with an electric mixer until smooth.
- Mix the #1 and #2 ingredients together with a wooden spoon.
- Pour into a greased 9 x 5 loaf pan and bake 55 to 60 minutes or until an inserted toothpick comes out clean.

Banana Bread with Almonds

Preheat oven to 350°

MAKES 1 LOAF

#1 Ingredients
2 cups all-purpose flour
1/2 teaspoon salt
2/3 cup sugar
1/2 teaspoon baking soda
1/2 teaspoon baking powder
2/3 cup almonds, sliced and
    toasted

#2 Ingredients
2 eggs, beaten
1/4 cup oil
1 cup buttermilk
1 1/2 cups bananas, mashed

- Mix the #1 ingredients together with a fork. Mix the #2 ingredients together with a wire whisk.
- Mix the #1 and #2 ingredients together with a wooden spoon.
- Pour into a greased 9 x 5 loaf pan and bake 50 minutes or until an inserted toothpick comes out clean.

Banana Bread with Cream Cheese

Preheat oven to 350°

MAKES 1 LOAF

#1 Ingredients
2 cups all-purpose flour
3 teaspoons baking powder
3/4 teaspoon salt
2/3 cup sugar
1/2 teaspoon baking soda

#2 Ingredients
1/3 cup melted butter or margarine
2 eggs, beaten
2 tablespoons buttermilk
1 1/2 cups bananas, mashed
1/2 cup soft cream cheese, room temperature

- Mix the #1 ingredients together with a wire whisk. Mix the #2 ingredients together with an electric mixer until smooth.
- Mix the #1 and the #2 ingredients together using a wooden spoon.
- Pour into a greased 9 x 5 loaf pan and bake 50 to 60 minutes or until an inserted toothpick comes out clean.

Peanutty Banana Bread

Preheat oven to 350°

MAKES 1 LOAF

#1 Ingredients
2 cups all-purpose flour
3 teaspoons baking powder
1 teaspoon baking soda
1/2 teaspoon salt
1 cup sugar
2/3 cup peanuts, chopped

#2 Ingredients
1 cup bananas, mashed
1 egg, beaten
1/4 cup oil
1/2 cup creamy peanut butter
3/4 cup milk

- Mix the #1 ingredients together with a wire whisk. Mix the #2 ingredients with an electric mixer until well blended.
- Mix the #1 and the #2 ingredients together using a wooden spoon.
- Pour into a well greased 9 x 5 loaf pan and bake 50 to 60 minutes or until an inserted toothpick comes out clean.

Banana Strawberry Bread

Preheat oven to 375°

MAKES 1 LOAF

#1 Ingredients
2 cups all-purpose flour
3 teaspoons baking powder
1 teaspoon salt
1/2 cup sugar
1/2 teaspoon baking soda

#2 Ingredients
1/4 cup melted butter or margarine
1 1/4 cups buttermilk
2 eggs, beaten
1 cup frozen strawberries in syrup, defrosted (plus 3 tablespoons of the liquid)
1 1/2 cups bananas, mashed

- Mix the #1 ingredients together with a wire whisk. Mix the #2 ingredients together with a fork.
- Mix the #1 and #2 ingredients together with a wooden spoon.
- Pour into a 9 x 5 greased loaf pan and bake 60 minutes or until an inserted toothpick comes out clean.

Variation: Use 1 cup fresh strawberries, sliced. Cover with 2 tablespoons sugar and chill for two hours and use 3 tablespoons of the liquid. Or use 1 cup blueberries, fresh or frozen and 3 tablespoons of the liquid. Same directions as the strawberries.

Ginger and Banana Loaf

Preheat oven to 375°

MAKES 1 LOAF

#1 Ingredients
2 cups all-purpose flour
3 teaspoons baking powder
1 teaspoon salt
1/2 cup brown sugar, packed
1/2 teaspoon baking soda
1 teaspoon cinnamon
2 teaspoons ground ginger
1/4 teaspoon ground cloves
1/2 cup golden raisins

#2 Ingredients
1/2 cup milk
1/4 cup melted butter or margarine
2 eggs, beaten
1/4 cup dark molasses
1/2 cup bananas, mashed

- Mix the #1 ingredients together with a fork. Mix the #2 ingredients together with an electric mixer until smooth.
- Mix the #1 and #2 ingredients together with a wooden spoon.
- Pour into a greased 9 x 5 loaf pan and bake 60 minutes or until an inserted toothpick comes out clean.

Monkey Bread

Preheat oven to 350°

MAKES 1 LOAF

#1 Ingredients
2 cups all-purpose flour
2 teaspoons baking powder
1 teaspoon salt
3/4 cup sugar
1/2 teaspoon baking soda
1/2 cup slivered almonds

#2 Ingredients
1 cup bananas, mashed
1/3 cup oil
1/4 cup buttermilk
2 eggs, beaten

- Mix the #1 ingredients together with a fork. Mix the #2 ingredients together with an electric mixer until smooth.
- Mix the #1 and #2 ingredients together with a wooden spoon.
- Pour into a greased 9 x 5 loaf pan and bake 50 to 60 minutes or until an inserted toothpick comes out clean.

Madeira Bread

Preheat oven to 375°

MAKES 1 LOAF

#1 Ingredients
2 cups all-purpose flour
3 teaspoons baking powder
1 teaspoon salt
1/2 cup sugar
1/2 teaspoon baking soda
1/2 teaspoon ground nutmeg
1/2 teaspoon ground ginger
1 1/2 teaspoons caraway seeds

#2 Ingredients
1/2 cup milk
1/4 cup melted butter or margarine
1 egg, beaten
1/2 cup sherry or Madeira

- Mix the #1 ingredients together with a wire whisk. Mix the #2 ingredients together with a wire whisk.
- Mix the #1 and #2 ingredients together with a wooden spoon.
- Pour into a greased 9 x 5 loaf pan and bake 50 to 60 minutes or until an inserted toothpick comes out clean.

Grape Nut Quickbread

Preheat oven to 375°

MAKES 1 LOAF

#1 Ingredients
2 cups all-purpose flour
3 teaspoons baking powder
1 teaspoon salt
2/3 cup sugar
1 cup Grape Nuts cereal

#2 Ingredients
1/3 cup melted butter or margarine
2 cups milk
3 eggs, beaten

#3 Ingredient
3 tablespoons Grape Nuts cereal

#4 Ingredient
1 egg, beaten

- Mix #1 ingredients together with a fork. Mix #2 ingredients together with a wire whisk.
- Mix the #1 and #2 ingredients together with a wooden spoon.
- Pour into a 9 x 5 greased loaf pan and sprinkle the top with the #3 ingredient.
- Brush with the #4 ingredient and bake 60 minutes or until an inserted toothpick comes out clean.

Carrot Zucchini Garden Bread

Preheat oven to 350°

MAKES 1 LOAF

#1 Ingredients
1 3/4 cups all-purpose flour
3 teaspoons baking powder
1/2 teaspoon baking soda
1/2 teaspoon salt
1 cup sugar
1 teaspoon cinnamon

#2 Ingredients
1/2 cup oil
2 eggs, beaten
1 teaspoon vanilla
1 cup zucchini, grated and drained
  on a paper towel
1 cup carrots, grated

- Mix the #1 ingredients together with a wire whisk. Mix the #2 ingredients together with a fork.
- Mix the #1 and the #2 ingredients together with a wooden spoon.
- Pour into a greased 9 x 5 loaf pan and bake 50 to 60 minutes or until an inserted toothpick comes out clean.

Variation: If you don't want to use both carrots and zucchini, use 2 cups either the carrots or zucchini.

The Best Ever Chocolate Tea Bread

Preheat oven to 350°

MAKES 1 LOAF

#1 Ingredients
1½ cups all-purpose flour
¼ teaspoon baking powder
¾ teaspoon salt
1 teaspoon baking soda
½ cup sugar
⅓ cup cocoa powder

#2 Ingredients
½ cup melted butter
2 eggs, beaten
½ cup applesauce
⅓ cup water
1 cup chocolate chips

#3 Ingredient
1 tablespoon powdered sugar

- Mix the #1 ingredients together with a wire whisk. Mix the #2 ingredients together with a fork.
- Mix the #1 and #2 ingredients together with a wooden spoon.
- Pour into a greased 9 x 5 loaf pan and bake for 55 to 60 minutes or until an inserted toothpick comes out clean.
- Dust with the #3 ingredient.

Butterscotch Tea Bread

Preheat oven to 350°

MAKES 1 LOAF

#1 Ingredients
2 cups all-purpose flour
1½ teaspoons baking powder
1 teaspoon salt
1 teaspoon baking soda
¼ cup sugar
⅛ teaspoon nutmeg
⅛ teaspoon cinnamon
1 cup pecans, chopped

#2 Ingredients
3 tablespoons melted butter
2 eggs, beaten
1 cup buttermilk
1 cup butterscotch chips

- Mix the #1 ingredients together with a wire whisk. Mix the #2 ingredients together with a fork.
- Mix the #1 and #2 ingredients together with a wooden spoon.
- Pour into a greased 9 x 5 inch loaf pan and bake for 55 to 60 minutes or until an inserted toothpick comes out clean.

John's Gumdrop Bread

Preheat oven to 350°

MAKES 1 LOAF

#1 Ingredients
3 cups all-purpose flour
3½ teaspoons baking powder
1 teaspoon salt
¾ cup sugar
1 cup small Gummy Bears
½ cup nuts, chopped (your
  choice)

#2 Ingredients
2 tablespoons melted butter
1 cup milk
1 egg, beaten

- Mix the #1 ingredients together with a fork. Mix the #2 ingredients together with a wire whisk.
- Mix the #1 and #2 ingredients together with a wooden spoon.
- Pour into a greased 9 x 5 loaf pan and bake for 55 to 60 minutes or until an inserted toothpick comes out clean.

Orange Crush Pop Bread

THIS WAS DISCOVERED ON A CAMPING TRIP WHEN WATER
WAS SCARCE, BUT WE HAD LOTS OF POP

Preheat oven to 400°

MAKES 1 LOAF

#1 Ingredients
3 cups all-purpose flour
3 teaspoons baking powder
1 teaspoon salt
½ teaspoon baking soda

#2 Ingredients
¼ cup sugar
1 12-ounce can orange soda pop
¼ cup melted butter or margarine

- Mix the #1 ingredients together with a wire whisk. Mix the #2 ingredients together with a wire whisk.
- Mix the #1 and #2 ingredients together with a wooden spoon. Pour into a greased 9 x 5 loaf pan and bake 55 to 60 minutes or until an inserted toothpick comes out clean.

Variation: Since then I've tried grape, root beer, and cola and all are quite good. Use 1 12-ounce can of soda.

Chapter 15

WHOLE GRAIN LOAF BREADS

Quick Onion Rye with Caraway Seeds
Preheat oven to 400°
MAKES 1 LOAF

#1 Ingredients
1 cup rye flour
1 cup all-purpose flour
3 teaspoons baking powder
1 teaspoon salt
1/2 teaspoon baking soda
2 tablespoons caraway seeds
1/2 cup green onion, sliced thin

#2 Ingredients
1 cup buttermilk
1/4 cup melted butter or margarine
1 egg, beaten

• Mix the #1 ingredients together with a fork. Mix the #2 ingredients together with a wire whisk.
• Mix the #1 and #2 ingredients together with a wooden spoon.
• Pour into a greased 9 x 5 loaf pan and bake 60 minutes or until an inserted toothpick comes out clean.

Casserole Millet Bread with Herbs
Preheat oven to 375°
MAKES 2 LOAVES OR 1 CASSEROLE LOAF

#1 Ingredients
1/2 cup millet flour
31/2 cups all-purpose flour
3 teaspoons baking powder
1 teaspoon salt
1/2 teaspoon baking soda
1 teaspoon each, dried, of the
    following: dill weed, cumin seed,
    basil, and Italian seasoning

#2 Ingredients
1/2 cup buttermilk
1/2 cup butter or margarine,
    melted
3 eggs, beaten
11/2 cups water

• Mix the #1 ingredients together with a wire whisk. Mix the #2 ingredients together with a wire whisk.
• Mix the #1 and #2 ingredients together with a wooden spoon.
• Pour into a greased 2-quart oven proof casserole dish and bake 55 minutes or until an inserted toothpick comes out clean.

Quick Pumpernickel

Preheat oven to 400°

MAKES 1 LOAF

#1 Ingredient
2 large potatoes, peeled and finely
  diced

#2 Ingredients
1/2 cup rye flour
1/2 cup cornmeal
1/2 cup whole wheat flour
1/2 cup all-purpose flour
3 teaspoons baking powder
1 teaspoon salt
1/2 cup sugar
1 tablespoon caraway seeds

#3 Ingredients
1/2 cup milk
1/2 cup potato water
1/8 cup melted butter or margarine
1 egg, beaten
3 tablespoons dark molasses

- Cook and mash the #1 ingredient and set aside (save 1/2 cup potato water).
- Mix the #2 ingredients together with a wire whisk. Mix the #3 ingredients together with a wire whisk.
- Mix the #1, #2, and #3 ingredients together with a wooden spoon.
- Pour into a greased 9 x 5 loaf pan and bake 60 minutes or until an inserted toothpick comes out clean.

Carrot and Millet Loaf

Preheat oven to 350°

MAKES 1 LOAF

#1 Ingredients
1 cup millet flour (found in health
  food stores)
1 cup all-purpose flour
3 teaspoons baking powder
1 teaspoon salt
1/2 teaspoon baking soda

#2 Ingredients
2/3 cup buttermilk
1/4 cup melted butter or margarine
3 eggs, beaten
1 cup carrots, grated

- Mix the #1 ingredients together with a wire whisk. Mix the #2 ingredients together with a fork.
- Mix the #1 and #2 ingredients together with a wooden spoon.
- Pour into a greased 9 x 5 loaf pan and bake 50 to 60 minutes or until an inserted toothpick comes out clean.

Buckwheat and Sesame Seed Quickbread

Preheat oven to 400°

MAKES 1 LOAF

#1 Ingredients
1 cup buckwheat flour
1 cup all-purpose flour
3 teaspoons baking powder
1 teaspoon salt
1/2 teaspoon baking soda
4 tablespoons toasted sesame
seeds

#2 Ingredients
1/4 cup melted butter or margarine
1 cup buttermilk
1 egg, beaten
2 tablespoons dark molasses

#3 Ingredient
2 tablespoons toasted sesame
seeds

#4 Ingredient
1 egg, beaten

- Mix the #1 ingredients together with a wire whisk. Mix the #2 ingredients together with a wire whisk.
- Mix the #1 and #2 ingredients together with a wooden spoon.
- Pour into a greased 9 x 5 loaf pan and top with the #3 ingredient.
- Brush top with the #4 ingredient and bake 55 to 60 minutes or until an inserted toothpick comes out clean.

Whole Wheat Honey Bread

Preheat oven to 350°

MAKES 1 LOAF

#1 Ingredients
2 cups whole wheat flour
1 cup all-purpose flour
4 teaspoons baking powder
1 teaspoon salt

#2 Ingredients
1 cup honey
1 cup milk
2 tablespoons oil
1 egg, beaten

- Mix the #1 ingredients together with a wire whisk. Mix the #2 ingredients together with a wire whisk.
- Mix the #1 and the #2 ingredients together with a wooden spoon.
- Pour into a greased 9 x 5 loaf pan and bake 50 to 60 minutes or until an inserted toothpick comes out clean.

Quick Buttermilk Oatmeal Loaf

Preheat oven to 400°

MAKES 1 LOAF

#1 Ingredients
3 cups all-purpose flour
1/2 cup quick rolled oats
1 teaspoon salt
3 teaspoons baking powder
1 teaspoon baking soda

#2 Ingredients
2 1/4 cups buttermilk
2 eggs, beaten

#3 Ingredient
1 stick butter, divided in half and melted

- Mix the #1 ingredients together with a wire whisk. Mix the #2 ingredients together with a wire whisk.
- Mix the #1 and #2 ingredients together with a wooden spoon.
- Pour half the #3 ingredients into a 9 x 5 loaf pan and roll around, coating all sides.
- Pour the batter into the loaf pan and pour the remaining #3 ingredient on top.
- Bake 30 minutes or until an inserted toothpick comes out clean.

A Quick and Healthy Bread

Preheat oven to 375°

MAKES 1 LOAF

#1 Ingredients
1 1/4 cups bran cereal
1 1/4 cups soy flour
1/8 cup flax seed (found in health food stores)
1/2 teaspoon salt or to taste
3 teaspoons baking powder
2 tablespoons wheat germ

#2 Ingredients
1 2/3 cups milk
2 eggs, beaten
2 tablespoons olive oil

- Mix the #1 ingredients with a wire whisk. Mix the #2 ingredients with a wire whisk.
- Mix the #1 and #2 ingredients together.
- Pour into a greased 9 x 5 loaf pan and bake 45 to 50 minutes or until an inserted toothpick comes out clean.

Alabama Rice Bread

Preheat oven to 400°

MAKES 1 LOAF

#1 Ingredients
1 cup uncooked minute rice
1 tablespoon butter

#2 Ingredients
1/2 cup cornmeal
3 teaspoons baking powder
1 teaspoon salt

#3 Ingredients
1 cup milk
3 eggs, beaten

- Cook the #1 ingredients together following package directions and set aside.
- Mix the #2 ingredients together with a wire whisk. Mix the #3 ingredients together with a wire whisk.
- Mix the #1, #2, and #3 ingredients together with a wooden spoon.
- Pour into a greased 9 x 5 loaf pan and bake 60 minutes or until an inserted toothpick comes out clean.

Whole Wheat Quickbread

Preheat oven to 350°

MAKES 1 LOAF

#1 Ingredients
1 cup whole wheat flour
1 cup all-purpose flour
3 teaspoons baking powder
1/4 teaspoon salt

#2 Ingredients
1 egg, beaten
1 cup milk
2 tablespoons oil

- Mix the #1 ingredients together with a wire whisk. Mix the #2 ingredients together with a wire whisk.
- Mix the #1 and #2 ingredients together with a wooden spoon.
- Pour into a greased 9 x 5 loaf pan and bake 45 to 50 minutes or until an inserted toothpick comes out clean.

Variation: you can also add toasted wheat germ. Add 1/2 cup to the #1 ingredients.

7-Grain Quickbread

Preheat oven to 400°

MAKES 1 LOAF

#1 Ingredients
1/4 cup oat flour
1/4 cup whole wheat flour
1/4 cup bulghur wheat flour
1/4 cup rye
1/4 cup soy flour
1/4 cup corn flour
4 teaspoons baking powder
1 teaspoon salt
1/2 teaspoon baking soda
1 tablespoon wheat germ
1 tablespoon sunflower seeds, chopped
1 tablespoon toasted sesame seeds
1 tablespoon poppy seeds

#2 Ingredients
1/4 cup melted butter or margarine
1 1/8 cups buttermilk
2 eggs, beaten

- Mix the #1 ingredients together with a wire whisk. Mix the #2 ingredients together with a wire whisk.
- Mix the #1 and #2 ingredients together with a wooden spoon.
- Pour into a 9 x 5 greased loaf pan and bake 60 minutes or until an inserted toothpick comes out clean.

Granola Bread

Preheat oven to 400°

MAKES 1 LOAF

#1 Ingredients
2 cups all-purpose flour
3 teaspoons baking powder
1 teaspoon salt
1/2 teaspoon baking soda
1 cup granola cereal

#2 Ingredients
1/2 cup sugar
1/4 cup melted butter or margarine
1 1/2 cups buttermilk
2 eggs, beaten
2 tablespoons water

- Mix #1 ingredients together with a fork. Mix #2 ingredients together with a wire whisk.
- Mix the #1 and #2 ingredients together with a wooden spoon.
- Pour into a 9 x 5 greased loaf pan and bake 60 minutes or until an inserted toothpick comes out clean.

Logan Bread

Preheat oven to 350°

MAKES 1 LOAF

#1 Ingredients
2 cups whole wheat flour
2/3 cup dark brown sugar, packed
4 teaspoons baking powder
1 teaspoon salt
1/2 cup wheat germ
4 tablespoons toasted sesame seeds

#2 Ingredients
1/2 cup honey
1/2 cup milk
1/4 cup butter or margarine, melted
1 egg, beaten
1/2 cup dark molasses

- Mix the #1 ingredients together with a wire whisk. Mix the #2 ingredients together with an electric mixer until smooth.
- Mix the #1 and #2 ingredients together with a wooden spoon.
- Pour into a greased 9 x 5 loaf pan and bake 60 minutes or until an inserted toothpick comes out clean.

Boston Brown Bread

GOES GREAT WITH SOFT CREAM CHEESE

Preheat oven to 350°

MAKES 2 LOAVES

#1 Ingredients
1 cup cornmeal
1 cup rye flour
1 cup whole wheat flour
1 teaspoon salt
1 teaspoon baking soda
1 cup raisins

#2 Ingredients
2 1/2 cups milk with 2 1/2 tablespoons vinegar or lemon juice stirred in
3/4 cup molasses
2 tablespoons melted butter

- Mix the #1 ingredients together with a wire whisk. Mix the #2 ingredients together with a wire whisk.
- Mix the #1 and the #2 ingredients together with a wooden spoon.
- Spray two, clean 1 pound coffee cans with cooking spray and pour equal amounts of the batter into the cans. Cover tightly with foil.
- Place the filled cans in a turkey roaster and fill the roaster half full with boiling water. If you don't have a turkey roaster do the same thing with a deep baking dish or pan.
- Cover tightly with foil and bake 1 1/2 hours or until an inserted toothpick comes out clean.

Bran and Apricot Loaf

Preheat oven to 400°

MAKES 1 LOAF

#1 Ingredients
1½ cups all-purpose flour
3¼ teaspoons baking powder
1 teaspoon salt
1 cup dried apricots, very finely
    chopped
1½ cups bran cereal
½ cup sugar

#2 Ingredients
⅓ cup melted butter or margarine
1 cup milk
2 eggs, beaten

- Mix the #1 ingredients together with a fork. Mix the #2 ingredients together with a wire whisk.
- Mix the #1 and #2 ingredients together with a wooden spoon.
- Pour into a 9 x 5 greased loaf pan and bake 50 to 60 minutes or until an inserted toothpick comes out clean.

Raisin Whole Wheat Bread

Preheat oven to 350°

MAKES 1 LOAF

#1 Ingredients
2½ cups whole wheat flour
½ cup all-purpose flour
1½ teaspoons baking soda
4 teaspoons baking powder
1 teaspoon salt
½ cup raisins
½ cup sugar

#2 Ingredients
1½ cups buttermilk
½ cup molasses
2 eggs, beaten

- Mix the #1 ingredients together with a wire whisk. Mix the #2 ingredients together using a wire whisk.
- Mix the #1 and #2 ingredients together.
- Pour into a greased 9 x 5 loaf pan and bake 50 to 60 minutes or until an inserted toothpick comes out clean.

Chapter 16

ROLLED BISCUITS

Always spray your cooking surface with cooking spray.

When making rolled biscuits you want a nice smooth dough, not sticky. In these recipes I use ¾ cup milk, the other ingredients have been adjusted for this. Flour can be temperamental so there are times when you will need more milk or flour; just keep close at hand and add if needed.

If you don't want to use buttermilk, just omit the baking soda and use regular milk in place of the buttermilk. Or vice versa. Add ¾ cup buttermilk to the #3 ingredients and ½ teaspoon baking soda with the #1 ingredients.

The serving size for the biscuits is based on a 2½-inch biscuit cutter The number of biscuits will depend on the size, shape, or cutter you choose.

Simple Biscuits

Preheat oven to 400°

MAKES 12 BISCUITS

#1 Ingredients
2 cups all-purpose flour
3 teaspoons baking powder
½ teaspoon salt

#2 Ingredient
¼ cup soft butter

#3 Ingredient
¾ cup milk

- Mix the #1 ingredients together with a wire whisk. Mix the #1 and #2 ingredients together with a pastry blender until crumbly.
- Mix the #3 ingredient with the #1 and #2 ingredients using a wooden spoon. Place your dough on a floured surface, flour your hands, and knead 5 times.
- Flour your rolling pin and roll out to ½ inch thick. Cut into biscuits and place on a cookie sheet. Bake for 20 to 30 minutes or until golden brown.

Biscuits with Your Homemade Mix

Preheat oven to 400°

MAKES 12 BISCUITS

#1 Ingredients: Homemade Biscuit Mix
9 cups all-purpose flour
1/4 cup baking powder
1 tablespoon salt

#2 Ingredient
1/4 cup soft butter or margarine

#3 Ingredient
3/4 cup milk

Use: #1 Ingredient
2 cups homemade biscuit mix

- Mix the #1 and #2 ingredients together using a pastry blender, until crumbly. Mix the #3 ingredient with the #1 and #2 ingredients using a wooden spoon. Place your dough on a floured surface, flour your hands and knead 5 times.
- Flour your rolling pin, roll out to 1/2 inch thick. Cut into biscuits, and place on a cookie sheet. Bake for 15 to 20 minutes or until golden brown.

Tall Biscuits

Preheat oven to 400°

MAKES 12 BISCUITS

#1 Ingredients
2 1/2 cups all-purpose flour
4 1/2 teaspoons baking powder
2 tablespoons sugar
1 teaspoon salt
3/4 teaspoon cream of tartar

#2 Ingredient
1/3 cup soft butter or margarine

#3 Ingredients
3/4 cup milk
1 egg, beaten

- Mix the #1 ingredients together with a wire whisk. Mix the #1 and #2 ingredients together with a pastry blender until crumbly.
- Mix the #3 ingredients together with a wire whisk. Mix the #1, #2 and #3 ingredients together using a wooden spoon. Place your dough on a floured surface, flour your hands, and knead 5 times.
- Flour your rolling pin and roll out to 1/2 inch thick. Cut into biscuits and place on a cookie sheet. Bake for 20 to 30 minutes or until golden brown.

Sage and Onion Biscuits

Preheat oven to 400°

MAKES 12 BISCUITS

#1 Ingredients
2 cups all-purpose flour
3 teaspoons baking powder
1 teaspoon salt

#2 Ingredient
1/4 cup soft butter or margarine

#3 Ingredients
3/4 cup milk
2 tablespoons fresh rubbed sage, chopped
1/2 cup green onions, sliced thin (tops only)

- Mix the #1 ingredients together with a wire whisk. Mix the #1 and #2 ingredients together using a pastry blender, until crumbly.
- Mix the #3 ingredients with the #1 and #2 ingredients using a wooden spoon. Place your dough on a floured surface, flour your hands, and knead 5 times.
- Flour your rolling pin and roll out to 1/2 inch thick. Cut into biscuits and place on a cookie sheet. Bake for 15 to 20 minutes or until golden brown.

French Fried Onion Biscuits

Preheat oven to 400°

MAKES 12 BISCUITS

#1 Ingredients
2 cups all-purpose flour
3 teaspoons baking powder
1 teaspoon salt

#2 Ingredient
1/4 cup soft butter or margarine

#3 Ingredient
3/4 cup milk
1/2 cup French fried onions, crumbled
1 cup longhorn cheese, shredded

- Mix the #1 ingredients together with a wire whisk. Mix the #1 and #2 ingredients together using a pastry blender, until crumbly.
- Mix the #1, #2 and #3 ingredients together using a wooden spoon. Place your dough on a floured surface, flour your hands, and knead 5 times.
- Flour your rolling pin and roll out to 1/2 inch thick. Cut into biscuits and place on a cookie sheet. Bake for 15 to 20 minutes or until golden brown.

Mozzarella Cheese Biscuits

Preheat oven to 400°

MAKES 12 BISCUITS

#1 Ingredients
2 cups all-purpose flour
3 teaspoons baking powder
1 teaspoon salt
1/2 teaspoon baking soda
1 teaspoon dried oregano
1/4 teaspoon garlic powder

#2 Ingredient
1/4 cup soft butter or margarine

#3 Ingredients
3/4 cup buttermilk
2 cups mozzarella cheese,
   shredded

- Mix the #1 ingredients together with a wire whisk. Mix the #1 and #2 ingredients together with a pastry blender until crumbly.
- Mix the #3 ingredients with the #1 and #2 ingredients using a wooden spoon. Place your dough on a floured surface, flour your hands, and knead 5 times.
- Flour your rolling pin and roll out to 1/2 inch thick. Cut into biscuits and place on a cookie sheet. Bake for 15 to 20 minutes or until golden brown.

Variation: You can use the same amount of a different cheese: cheddar, Colby, Swiss, American, jalapeño, Monterey Jack, and longhorn, just to name a few.

Wheat Germ and Cheese Biscuits

Preheat oven to 400°

MAKES 12 BISCUITS

#1 Ingredients
2 cups all-purpose flour
3 teaspoons baking powder
1 teaspoon salt
1/2 cup toasted wheat germ

#3 Ingredients
3/4 cup milk
1 1/2 cup provolone cheese,
   shredded

#2 Ingredient
1/4 cup soft butter or margarine

- Mix the #1 ingredients together with a wire whisk. Mix the #1 and #2 ingredients together using a pastry blender, until crumbly.
- Mix the #1, #2 and #3 ingredients together using a wooden spoon. Place your dough on a floured surface, flour your hands, and knead 5 times.
- Flour your rolling pin and roll out to 1/2 inch thick. Cut into biscuits and place on a cookie sheet. Bake for 15 to 20 minutes or until golden brown.

Chili Cheese Biscuits

Preheat oven to 400°

MAKES 6 LARGE BISCUITS

#1 Ingredients
2 cups all-purpose flour
4 teaspoons baking powder
1 teaspoon salt
1/2 teaspoon chili powder
1/2 teaspoon cumin

#2 Ingredient
1/4 cup soft butter or margarine

#3 Ingredients
3/4 cup heavy cream
1 cup jalapeño-flavored cheese, or
   a milder cheese, shredded

- Mix the #1 ingredients together with a wire whisk. Mix the #1 and #2 ingredients together with a pastry blender until crumbly.
- Mix the #3 ingredients with the #1 and #2 ingredients using a wooden spoon. Place your dough on a floured surface, flour your hands, and knead 5 times.
- Flour your rolling pin and roll out to 1/2 inch thick. Cut into extra large biscuits and place on a cookie sheet. Bake for 20 to 25 minutes or until golden brown.

Tomato Cheese Biscuits

Preheat oven to 400°

MAKES 12 BISCUITS

#1 Ingredients
2 cups all-purpose flour
3 teaspoons baking powder
1 teaspoon salt
1/2 teaspoon baking soda

#2 Ingredient
1/4 cup soft butter or margarine

#3 Ingredients
3/4 cup tomato juice
1/2 cup onion, very finely diced
2 cups provolone cheese,
   shredded
2 tablespoons green bell pepper,
   diced very small

- Mix all the #1 ingredients together with a wire whisk. Mix the #1 and #2 ingredients together with a pastry blender until crumbly.
- Mix the #3 ingredients with the #1 and #2 ingredients using a wooden spoon. Place your dough on a floured surface, flour your hands, and knead 5 times.
- Flour your rolling pin and roll out to 1/2 inch thick. Cut into biscuits and place on a cookie sheet. Bake for 15 to 20 minutes or until golden brown.

Tiny Shrimp Biscuits

FOR A LIST OF OTHER INGREDIENTS, SEE **VARIATIONS** BELOW.

Preheat oven to 400°

MAKES 12 BISCUITS

#1 Ingredients
2 cups all-purpose flour
3 teaspoons baking powder
1 teaspoon salt

#2 Ingredient
1/4 cup soft butter or margarine

#3 Ingredients
3/4 cup milk
1 6-ounce can tiny shrimp,
   drained and chopped
2 cups mozzarella cheese,
   shredded

- Mix the #1 ingredients together with a wire whisk. Mix the #1 and #2 ingredients together using a pastry blender, until crumbly.
- Mix the #1, #2 and #3 ingredients together using a wooden spoon. Place your dough on a floured surface, flour your hands, and knead 5 times.
- Flour your rolling pin and roll out to 1/2 inch thick. Cut into biscuits and place on a cookie sheet. Bake for 15 to 20 minutes or until golden brown.

Variations:
Just omit the tiny shrimp, and mozzarella cheese
and add the other ingredients.

TYPE OF BISCUITS	MIX WITH THE #1 INGREDIENTS
Bacon and Cheese	6 strips bacon, diced, fried, and drained, and add 2 cups American cheese, shredded
Chicken and Cheese	1 cup cooked chicken, diced small, and add 2 cups cheese, shredded (your choice)
Ham and Cheese	1 cup smoked ham and 2 cups Swiss cheese, shredded
Pepperoni and Cheese	3/4 cup pepperoni, diced small, and add 1 1/2 cups mozzarella cheese, shredded
Sausage and Cheese	1 cup mild sausage, ground, browned and drained, and add 1 1/2 cups mild cheddar cheese, shredded
Tuna and Cheese	1 6-ounce can tuna, packed in water and drained, and add 1 1/2 cups cheese, shredded (your choice)

Quick Pumpkin Biscuits

Preheat oven to 375°

MAKES 12 BISCUITS

#1 Ingredients
2 cups buttermilk pancake mix
2 tablespoons sugar
1½ teaspoons pumpkin pie spice

#2 Ingredient
⅔ cup canned pumpkin

#3 Ingredient
3 tablespoons milk

- Mix the #1 ingredients together with a wire whisk. Mix the #1 and #2 ingredients together with a pastry blender until crumbly. Add the #3 ingredients, one tablespoon at a time.
- Place your dough on a floured surface, flour your hands, and knead 5 times.
- Flour your rolling pin and roll out to ½ inch thick. Cut into biscuits and place on a cookie sheet. Bake for 20 to 30 minutes or until golden brown.

Peanut Butter Biscuits

WITH SOME JELLY ON TOP

Preheat oven to 400°

MAKES 12 BISCUITS

#1 Ingredients
2 cups all-purpose flour
3 teaspoons baking powder
1 teaspoon salt
½ teaspoon baking soda

#3 Ingredients
¾ cup buttermilk
½ cup chunky peanut butter
3 tablespoons peanuts, chopped small

#2 Ingredient
¼ cup soft butter or margarine

- Mix the #1 ingredients together with a wire whisk. Mix the #1 and #2 ingredients together with a pastry blender until crumbly. Mix the #3 ingredients together with an electric mixer until well blended.
- Mix the #1, #2, and #3 ingredients together using a wooden spoon. Place your dough on a floured surface, flour your hands, and knead 5 times.
- Flour your rolling pin and roll out to ½ inch thick. Cut into biscuits and place on a cookie sheet. Bake for 15 to 20 minutes or until golden brown.

Poppy Seed and Buttermilk Biscuits

Preheat oven to 400°

MAKES 12 BISCUITS

#1 Ingredients
2 cups all-purpose flour
2 tablespoons poppy seeds
3 teaspoons baking powder
1/2 teaspoon baking soda
1/2 teaspoon salt

#2 Ingredient
1/4 cup soft butter or margarine

#3 Ingredient
1 cup buttermilk

- Mix the #1 ingredients together with a wire whisk. Mix the #1 and #2 ingredients together with a pastry blender until crumbly.
- Mix the #1, #2, and #3 ingredients together using a wooden spoon. Place your dough on a floured surface, flour your hands, and knead 5 times.
- Flour your rolling pin and roll out to 1/2 inch thick. Cut into biscuits and place on a cookie sheet. Bake for 20 to 30 minutes or until golden brown.

Variation: Add 3 tablespoons of toasted sesame seeds to the #1 ingredients and 1 tablespoon toasted sesame oil (optional) to the #3 ingredient. The same amount of any other kind of seed can be used. Mix with the #1 ingredients.

Wheat Germ and Buttermilk Biscuits with Whole Wheat

Preheat oven to 400°

MAKES 12 BISCUITS

#1 Ingredients
1 cup whole wheat
1 cup all-purpose flour
3 teaspoons baking powder
1 teaspoon salt
1/2 teaspoon baking soda
1/2 cup toasted wheat germ

#2 Ingredient
1/4 cup soft butter or margarine

#3 Ingredient
3/4 cup buttermilk

- Mix the #1 ingredients together with a wire whisk. Mix the #1 and #2 ingredients together with a pastry blender until crumbly.
- Mix the #1, #2, and #3 ingredients together using a wooden spoon. Place your dough on a floured surface, flour your hands, and knead 5 times.
- Flour your rolling pin and roll out to 1/2 inch thick. Cut into biscuits and place on a cookie sheet. Bake for 15 to 20 minutes or until golden brown.

Salt Buttermilk Biscuits

DON'T LET THE NAME FOOL YOU, THEY ARE DELICIOUS AND YOU CAN
LEAVE THE SALT OFF THE TOP IF YOU PREFER.

Preheat oven to 400°

MAKES 12 BISCUITS

#1 Ingredients
2 cups all-purpose flour
2 tablespoons sugar
3 teaspoons baking powder
1/2 teaspoon baking soda
3/4 teaspoon cream of tartar

#2 Ingredients
1/4 cup soft cream cheese
2 tablespoons soft butter or
    margarine

#3 Ingredients
3/4 cup buttermilk
1 egg, beaten

#4 Ingredient
coarse salt

- Mix the #1 ingredients together with a wire whisk. Mix the #1 and #2 ingredients together with a pastry blender until crumbly.
- Mix the #1, #2, and #3 ingredients together using a wooden spoon. Place your dough on a floured surface, flour your hands, and knead 5 times.
- Flour your rolling pin and roll out to 1/2 inch thick. Cut into biscuits and place on a cookie sheet. Sprinkle with the #4 ingredient, and bake for 20 to 30 minutes or until golden brown.

Pepper Buttermilk Biscuits

Preheat oven to 400°

MAKES 12 BISCUITS

#1 Ingredients
2 cups all-purpose flour
3 teaspoons baking powder
1 teaspoon salt
1/2 teaspoon baking soda
1 teaspoon black pepper or to
    taste

#2 Ingredient
1/4 cup soft butter or margarine

#3 Ingredient
3/4 cup buttermilk

- Mix the #1 ingredients together with a wire whisk. Mix the #1 and #2 ingredients together with a pastry blender until crumbly.
- Mix the #1, #2, and #3 ingredients together using a wooden spoon. Place your dough on a floured surface, flour your hands, and knead 5 times.
- Flour your rolling pin and roll out to 1/2 inch thick. Cut into biscuits and place on a cookie sheet. Bake for 15 to 20 minutes or until golden brown.

Spicy Mustard and Chives Biscuits

Preheat oven to 375°

MAKES 12 BISCUITS

#1 Ingredients
2 cups all-purpose flour
3 teaspoons baking powder
1 teaspoon salt
1/2 teaspoon baking soda

#2 Ingredient
1/4 cup soft butter or margarine

#3 Ingredients
3/4 cup buttermilk
1 tablespoon spicy mustard (your choice)
1/4 cup fresh chives, sliced thin and packed
1 cup Swiss cheese, shredded

- Mix the #1 ingredients together with a wire whisk. Mix the #1 and #2 ingredients together with a pastry blender until crumbly.
- Mix the #1, #2, and #3 ingredients together using a wooden spoon. Place the dough on a floured surface, flour your hands, and knead 5 times.
- Flour your rolling pin and roll out to 1/2 inch thick. Cut into biscuits and place on a cookie sheet. Bake for 15 to 20 minutes or until golden brown.

Caraway Rye Buttermilk Biscuits with Onion

Preheat oven to 400°

MAKES 12 BISCUITS

#1 Ingredients
1 cup rye flour
1 cup all-purpose flour
3 teaspoons baking powder
1 teaspoon salt
1/2 teaspoon baking soda
2 tablespoons dried onion flakes
1 tablespoon caraway seeds

#2 Ingredient
1/4 cup soft butter or margarine

#3 Ingredient
3/4 cup buttermilk

- Mix the #1 ingredients together with a wire whisk. Mix the #1 and #2 ingredients together with a pastry blender until crumbly.
- Mix the #1, #2, and #3 ingredients together using a wooden spoon. Place your dough on a floured surface, flour your hands, and knead 5 times.
- Flour your rolling pin and roll out to 1/2 inch thick. Cut into biscuits and place on a cookie sheet. Bake for 15 to 20 minutes or until golden brown.

Loaded Cottage Cheese Buttermilk Biscuits

Preheat oven to 400°

MAKES 12 BISCUITS

#1 Ingredients
2 cups all-purpose flour
3 teaspoons baking powder
1 teaspoon salt
1/4 teaspoon baking soda

#2 Ingredient
1/4 cup soft butter or margarine

#3 Ingredients
2/3 cup buttermilk
1/2 cup large curd cottage cheese
1 tablespoon red bell pepper,
    diced very small
1 tablespoon green onions, diced
    very small
1 teaspoon poppy seeds
1 teaspoon toasted sesame seeds

- Mix the #1 ingredients together with a wire whisk. Mix the #1 and #2 ingredients together with a pastry blender until crumbly.
- Mix the #3 ingredients together with a fork. Mix the #1, #2, and #3 ingredients together with a wooden spoon. Place your dough on a floured surface, flour your hands, and knead 5 times.
- Flour your rolling pin and roll out to 1/2 inch thick. Cut into biscuits and place on a cookie sheet. Bake for 15 to 20 minutes or until golden brown.

Tex Mex Biscuits

Preheat oven to 400°

MAKES 12 BISCUITS

#1 Ingredients
2 cups all-purpose flour
3 teaspoons baking powder
1 teaspoon salt
1/2 teaspoon baking soda
1 tablespoon taco seasoning

#2 Ingredient
1/4 cup soft butter or margarine

#3 Ingredients
3/4 cup buttermilk
1/4 cup green onions, sliced thin
2 cups Monterey Jack cheese,
    shredded

- Mix the #1 ingredients together with a wire whisk. Mix the #1 and #2 ingredients together with a pastry blender until crumbly.
- Mix the #1, #2, and #3 ingredients together using a wooden spoon. Place your dough on a floured surface, flour your hands, and knead 5 times.
- Flour your rolling pin and roll out to 1/2 inch thick. Cut into biscuits and place on a cookie sheet. Bake for 15 to 20 minutes or until golden brown.

Cheese, Spinach, and Onion Biscuits

Preheat oven to 400°

MAKES 12 BISCUITS

#1 Ingredients
2 cups all-purpose flour
3 teaspoons baking powder
1 teaspoon salt
1/2 teaspoon baking soda
2 teaspoons dried onion flakes

#2 Ingredient
1/4 cup soft butter or margarine

#3 Ingredients
3/4 cup buttermilk
1/2 cup fresh spinach, coarsely
  chopped
2 cups Monterey Jack cheese,
  shredded

- Mix the #1 ingredients together with a wire whisk. Mix the #1 and #2 ingredients together with a pastry blender until crumbly.
- Mix the #1, #2, and #3 ingredients together using a wooden spoon. Place your dough on a floured surface, flour your hands, and knead 5 times.
- Flour your rolling pin and roll out to 1/2 inch thick. Cut into biscuits and place on a cookie sheet. Bake for 15 to 20 minutes or until golden brown.

Onion and Parmesan Buttermilk Biscuits

Preheat oven to 375°

MAKES 12 BISCUITS

#1 Ingredients
2 cups all-purpose flour
3 teaspoons baking powder
1 teaspoon salt
1/2 teaspoon baking soda
1/2 cup Parmesan cheese, grated
1/2 cup onion, diced small
1 tablespoon poppy seeds

#2 Ingredient
1/4 cup soft butter or margarine

#3 Ingredient
3/4 cup buttermilk

- Mix the #1 ingredients together with a wire whisk. Mix the #1 and #2 ingredients together with a pastry blender until crumbly.
- Mix the #1, #2, and #3 ingredients together with a wooden spoon. Place your dough on a floured surface, flour your hands, and knead 5 times.
- Flour your rolling pin and roll out to 1/2 inch thick. Cut into biscuits and place on a cookie sheet. Bake for 15 to 20 minutes or until golden brown.

Sun-Dried Tomato and Onion Buttermilk Biscuits

Preheat oven to 400°

MAKES 12 BISCUITS

#1 Ingredients
2 cups all-purpose flour
3 teaspoons baking powder
1/2 teaspoon baking soda
2 tablespoons onion, diced small
3 tablespoons fresh basil, chopped
1/2 teaspoon salt

#2 Ingredient
1/4 cup soft butter or margarine

#3 Ingredients
1 1/4 cups buttermilk
1/3 cup sun-dried tomatoes, diced small
2 cups cheddar cheese, shredded

- Mix the #1 ingredients together with a fork. Mix the #1 and #2 ingredients together with a pastry blender until crumbly.
- Mix the #3 ingredients with the #1 and #2 ingredients with a wooden spoon. Place your dough on a floured surface, flour your hands, and knead 5 times.
- Flour your rolling pin and roll out to 1/2 inch thick. Cut into biscuits and place on a cookie sheet. Bake for 20 to 30 minutes or until golden brown.

Variation: Add 1 tablespoon Italian seasoning to the #1 ingredients. You can also switch the cheese to mozzarella or a cheese of your choice.

Cinnamon Swirl Buttermilk Biscuits

Preheat oven to 400°

MAKES 12 BISCUITS

#1 Ingredients
2 cups all-purpose flour
3 teaspoons baking powder
1 teaspoon salt
1/4 teaspoon baking soda

#2 Ingredient
1/4 cup soft butter or margarine

#3 Ingredient
3/4 cup buttermilk

#4 Ingredient
1/4 cup melted butter

#5 Ingredient
2/3 cup cinnamon sugar

#6 Ingredients
1 cup powdered sugar
2 tablespoons milk or enough to
   make the sugar runny
1 teaspoon vanilla extract

- Mix the # 6 ingredients together with a fork and set aside. It should be runny.
- Mix the #1 ingredients together with a wire whisk. Mix the #1 and #2 ingredients together with a pastry blender until crumbly. Mix the #1, #2, and #3 ingredients together with a wooden spoon.
- Place your dough on a floured surface, flour your hands, and knead 5 times. Flour your rolling pin, and roll out to 1/4 inch thick. Brush the #4 ingredient covering the dough to 1/2 inch from the edge.
- Sprinkle the #5 ingredient evenly over the melted butter to 1/2 inch from the edge. Roll up the dough and pinch all edges shut. Cut into 1 inch thick pieces and place on a cookie sheet that has been sprayed with cooking spray.
- Bake for 25 to 30 minutes or until golden brown, drizzle with the #6 ingredients.

Chapter 17

DROP BISCUITS

Drop biscuits are one of the easiest thing to make, and require no kneading. In this chapter, different ingredients are listed in **Variations** following the basic recipe below.

Basic Drop Biscuits

Preheat oven to 400°

MAKES 12 BISCUITS

#1 Ingredients
2 cups all-purpose flour
3 teaspoons baking powder
1 teaspoon salt

#2 Ingredient
1/4 cup soft butter or margarine

#3 Ingredient
1 cup milk

- Mix the #1 ingredients together with a wire whisk. Mix the #1 and #2 ingredients with a pastry blender until crumbly.
- Mix the #1, #2, and #3 ingredients together with a wooden spoon until well mixed. The batter will be sticky.
- Drop by the heaping tablespoonful onto a greased cookie sheet, 1 inch apart, and bake 15 to 20 minutes or until golden brown.

Variations

TYPE OF DROP BISCUITS	TO BE MIXED WITH THE #1 INGREDIENTS	TO BE MIXED WITH THE #3 INGREDIENTS
Cheese and Cayenne	1 teaspoon cayenne pepper or to taste	2 cups sharp cheddar cheese, shredded
Dill and Mustard	1 tablespoon fresh dill weed or 2 tablespoons, dried	2 tablespoons mustard of your choice
Garlic and Mozzarella Cheese	1 teaspoon garlic, minced	2 cups mozzarella cheese, shredded
Meats and Cheese		1 cup cooked meat, diced small and 2 cups cheese, shredded (your choice)
Sesame and Onion	3 tablespoon toasted sesame seeds	1/2 cup green onion, sliced thin
Whole Wheat and Cheese	Replace 1 cup all-purpose flour with 1 cup whole wheat flour	2 cups cheddar cheese, shredded

Variations: Sweet Drop Biscuits

TYPE OF DROP BISCUITS	TO BE MIXED WITH THE #1 INGREDIENTS	TO BE MIXED WITH THE #3 INGREDIENTS
Banana Nut	1/4 cup sugar	1 cup mashed bananas, 1 egg, beaten, 1/2 cup peanuts, chopped small
Chocolate Chip	1/2 cup sugar	1 cup chocolate chips
Date Nut	1/4 cup sugar	1 teaspoon vanilla, 1/3 cup dates, diced small, and 1/2 cup walnuts, chopped small
Ginger	1/2 teaspoon ginger, ground, 1/4 teaspoon cinnamon, 1/8 teaspoon cloves, ground, 1 teaspoon fresh orange zest, and 1/4 cup sugar	
Maple Nut		Use 2/3 cup milk, 1/3 cup maple syrup, 1 teaspoon maple extract and 1/2 cup walnuts, chopped small
Orange Marmalade	2 tablespoons sugar and 1/4 teaspoon fresh orange zest	1/2 cup orange marmalade
Pear	1/2 cup sugar	1/2 cup canned pears, diced small, 2/3 cup milk, and 1/3 cup juice from the canned pears
Pineapple	1/4 cup sugar	1/4 cup coconut, shredded, 1/2 cup pecans, chopped small. Omit the milk and use 1 cup pineapple juice and 1/2 cup crushed pineapple, drained
Raisin	1 teaspoon fresh orange zest, 1/2 teaspoon cinnamon, 1/4 teaspoon nutmeg, and 1/4 cup sugar	1 cup raisins

Chapter 18

CORN BREADS

The recipes in this chapter will call for one 9 x 5-inch loaf pan. If you prefer eating a square of corn bread instead of a slice, a 9 x 9 x 2-inch pan will work. Adjust the baking time from 30 to 35 minutes to 20 to 25 minutes.

Basic Corn Bread

Preheat oven to 350°

MAKES 1 LOAF

#1 Ingredients
1 cup corn meal
1 cup all-purpose flour
4 teaspoons baking powder
1 teaspoon salt

#2 Ingredients
1 cup milk
2 eggs, beaten
1/4 cup melted butter or margarine

- Mix the #1 ingredients together with a wire whisk. Mix the #2 ingredients together with a wire whisk.
- Mix the #1 and #2 ingredients together with a wooden spoon.
- Pour into a greased 9 x 5 pan. Bake 35 to 40 minutes or until an inserted toothpick comes out clean.

Homemade Corn Bread Mix

YOU CAN KEEP REFRIGERATED FOR UP TO 3 WEEKS

Preheat oven to 350°

MAKES 1 LOAF

#1 Ingredients
4 cups all-purpose flour
4 cups corn meal
1 3/4 cups non-fat dry milk
2 teaspoons salt

#2 Ingredient
1 3/4 cups butter-flavored shortening

- Mix ingredients with a wire whisk. Mix the #1 ingredients with the #2 ingredients with a pastry blender, put in an air-tight container and refrigerate.
- To use: 2 cups #1 ingredients mixture, 1 cup water, 1 egg, beaten.
- Mix the ingredients together with a wooden spoon. Pour into a greased 9 x 5 loaf pan and bake for 30 to 35 minutes or until an inserted toothpick comes out clean.

Southern-Style Corn Bread

Preheat oven to 375°

MAKES 1 LOAF

#1 Ingredients
1 cup corn meal
1 cup all-purpose flour
3 teaspoons baking powder
1/2 teaspoon salt
1/2 teaspoon baking soda

#2 Ingredients
2 eggs, beaten
1 15-ounce can of corn, drained
1/2 cup oil
3/4 cup sour cream

- Mix the #1 ingredients with a wire whisk. Mix the #2 ingredients with a wire whisk.
- Mix the #1 and #2 ingredients together with a wooden spoon.
- Pour into a greased 9 x 5 loaf pan and bake for 30 to 35 minutes or until an inserted toothpick comes out clean.

Hominy Corn Bread

Preheat oven to 350°

MAKES 1 LOAF

#1 Ingredients
1 cup corn meal
1 cup all-purpose flour
4 teaspoons baking powder
1 teaspoon salt

#2 Ingredients
1 cup milk
2 eggs, beaten
1/4 cup melted butter or margarine
1/2 cup yellow can of hominy, drained and chopped
1/4 cup green onion, sliced thin

- Mix the #1 ingredients together with a wire whisk. Mix the #2 ingredients together with a fork.
- Mix the #1 and #2 ingredients together with a wooden spoon.
- Pour into a greased 9 x 5 loaf pan and bake 35 to 40 minutes or until an inserted toothpick comes out clean.

Sage Corn Bread

Preheat oven to 400°

MAKES 1 LOAF

#1 Ingredients
1 cup corn meal
1 cup all-purpose flour
4 teaspoons baking powder
1/2 teaspoon salt
1 tablespoon fresh rubbed sage,
    chopped, or 2 tablespoons
    dried crushed sage leaf

#2 Ingredients
1 cup milk
2 eggs, beaten

- Mix the #1 ingredients together with a wire whisk. Mix the #2 ingredients together with a wire whisk.
- Mix the #1 and #2 ingredients together with a wooden spoon.
- Pour into a greased 9 x 5 loaf pan and bake for 35 to 40 minutes or until an inserted toothpick comes out clean.

Cheesy Cream-Style Corn Bread

Preheat oven to 375°

MAKES 1 LOAF

#1 Ingredients
1 cup corn meal
1 cup all-purpose flour
4 teaspoons baking powder
1 teaspoon salt
1/2 teaspoon baking soda

#2 Ingredients
1 cup buttermilk
2 eggs, beaten
1/4 cup melted butter or margarine
1/2 cup cream-style corn
1 cup sharp cheddar cheese,
    shredded

- Mix the #1 ingredients together with a wire whisk. Mix the #2 ingredients together a fork.
- Mix the #1 and #2 ingredients together with a wooden spoon.
- Pour into a greased 9 x 5 loaf pan and bake 35 to 40 minutes or until an inserted toothpick comes out clean.

Colorful Corn Bread

Preheat oven to 375°

MAKES 1 LOAF

#1 Ingredients
1 cup corn meal
1 cup all-purpose flour
4 teaspoons baking powder
1 teaspoon salt
1 teaspoon taco seasoning mix

#2 Ingredients
1 cup milk
2 eggs, beaten
1/4 cup melted butter or margarine
2 tablespoons red bell pepper, diced
2 tablespoons green bell pepper, diced
2 tablespoons onion, diced
1 cup Monterey Jack cheese, shredded

- Mix the #1 ingredients together with a wire whisk. Mix the #2 ingredients together with a fork.
- Mix the #1 and #2 ingredients together with a wooden spoon.
- Pour into a greased 9 x 5 loaf pan and bake 35 to 40 minutes or until an inserted toothpick comes out clean.

Chopped Broccoli and Cheese Corn Bread

Preheat oven to 375°

MAKES 1 LOAF

#1 Ingredients
1 cup corn meal
1 cup all-purpose flour
4 teaspoons baking powder
1 teaspoon salt

#2 Ingredients
1 cup milk
2 eggs, beaten
1/4 cup melted butter or margarine
1/3 cup frozen chopped broccoli, defrosted and drained
2 cups mozzarella cheese, shredded

- Mix the #1 ingredients together with a wire whisk. Mix the #2 ingredients together with a fork.
- Mix the #1 and #2 ingredients together with a wooden spoon.
- Pour into a greased 9 x 5 loaf pan and bake 35 to 40 minutes or until an inserted toothpick comes out clean.

Frito Corn Bread

Preheat oven to 400°

MAKES 1 LOAF

#1 Ingredients
1 cup yellow corn meal
1 cup all-purpose flour
1 tablespoon sugar
1 cup crushed chili cheese-flavored
   Fritos
1/2 cup mild cheddar cheese,
   shredded
3 teaspoons baking powder
1/2 teaspoon baking soda

#2 Ingredients
1 1/2 cup milk
2 eggs, beaten

- Mix the #1 ingredients together with a fork. Mix the #2 ingredients together with a wire whisk.
- Mix the #1 and #2 ingredients together with a wooden spoon.
- Pour into a greased 9 x 5 loaf pan and bake 30 to 35 minutes or until an inserted toothpick comes out clean.

Chili and Sour Cream Corn Bread

Preheat oven to 400°

MAKES 1 LOAF

#1 Ingredients
1 cup corn meal
1 cup all-purpose flour
3 teaspoons baking powder
1 teaspoon baking soda
1/2 cup jalapeño-flavored cheese,
   shredded

#2 Ingredients
1 cup cooked chili with beans,
   mashed with a fork
1 cup sour cream
1/2 cup soft butter or margarine
3 eggs, beaten

- Mix the #1 ingredients with a wire whisk. Mix the #2 ingredients with a wire whisk.
- Mix the #1 and #2 ingredients together with a wooden spoon.
- Pour into a greased 9 x 5 loaf pan and bake 30 to 35 minutes or until an inserted toothpick comes out clean.

Mexican Corn Bread

Preheat oven to 400°

MAKES 1 LOAF

#1 Ingredients
1 cup corn meal
1 cup all-purpose flour
3 teaspoons baking powder
1/2 teaspoon baking soda
1 teaspoon salt
1 teaspoon chili powder

#2 Ingredients
1 cup buttermilk
2 eggs, beaten
1 3-ounce can chopped green
    chilies, drained
1 cup cheddar cheese, shredded
3 tablespoons chopped pimentos,
    drained

- Mix the #1 ingredients together with a wire whisk. Mix the #2 ingredients together with a wire whisk.
- Mix the #1 and #2 ingredients together with a wooden spoon.
- Pour into a greased 9 x 5 pan and bake 35 to 40 minutes or until an inserted toothpick comes out clean.

Variation: Omit the canned chilies and use 1/2 tablespoon fresh jalapeño pepper, seeded and minced.

Brown Corn Bread

Preheat oven to 400°

MAKES 1 LOAF

#1 Ingredients
1 cup corn meal
2 cups all-purpose flour
4 teaspoons baking powder
1 teaspoon salt
2 tablespoons sugar
1/2 teaspoon baking soda

#2 Ingredients
1 12-ounce can dark beer
2 eggs, beaten
1/4 cup melted butter or margarine
1/2 cup dark molasses

- Mix the #1 ingredients together with a wire whisk. Mix the #2 ingredients together with a wire whisk.
- Mix the #1 and #2 ingredients together with a wooden spoon.
- Pour into a greased 9 x 5 loaf pan and bake 35 to 40 minutes or until an inserted toothpick comes out clean.

Sweet Corn Bread with a Surprise

Preheat oven to 375°

MAKES 1 LOAF

#1 Ingredients
1 cup yellow cornmeal
1 cup all-purpose flour
1/2 cup sugar
3 teaspoons baking powder
1/2 teaspoon cinnamon
1 cup coconut, shredded
1/2 teaspoon salt

#2 Ingredients
1 cup coconut milk or 1 cup half-and-half
2 eggs, beaten
1 teaspoon coconut extract

- Mix the #1 ingredients together with a wire whisk. Mix the #2 ingredients together with a wire whisk.
- Mix the #1 and #2 ingredients with a wooden spoon.
- Pour into a greased 9 x 5 loaf pan and bake for 35 to 40 minutes or until an inserted toothpick comes out clean.

Paraguay Corn Loaf

Preheat oven to 375°

MAKES 1 LOAF

#1 Ingredients
1 cup corn meal
1 cup all-purpose flour
4 teaspoons baking powder
1 teaspoon salt
1/2 teaspoon baking soda
1 tablespoon sugar

#2 Ingredients
1 cup buttermilk
3 eggs, beaten

1/4 cup melted butter or margarine
1/2 teaspoon liquid cayenne pepper
1 cup Monterey Jack cheese, shredded
1/2 cup onion, diced
1 cup cream-style corn
1/2 cup tomato, diced

#3 Ingredient
1/2 cup cracker crumbs

- Mix the #1 ingredients together with a wire whisk. Mix the #2 ingredients together with a wire whisk.
- Mix the #1 and #2 ingredients together with a wooden spoon.
- Pour into a greased 9 x 5 loaf pan and sprinkle the #3 ingredients over the top and bake 45 minutes or until an inserted toothpick comes out clean.

Chapter 19

SCONES

Scones must have a stiff dough, like the dough for biscuits but not as smooth. You can make scones without buttermilk, just use regular milk and omit the baking soda.

Basic Scone

TO ADD OTHER INGREDIENTS SEE **VARIATIONS** ON PAGE 191.

Preheat oven to 350°

MAKES 1 SCONE

#1 Ingredients
3 cups all-purpose flour
3 teaspoons baking powder
1 teaspoon salt
1/2 teaspoon baking soda

#2 Ingredient
1/2 cup soft butter or margarine

#3 Ingredients
1 egg, beaten
1 cup buttermilk

* Mix the #1 ingredients together with a wire whisk. Add the #2 ingredients to the #1 ingredients and mix with a pastry blender until crumbly.
* Mix the #3 ingredients together with a wire whisk. Mix the #1, #2, and #3 ingredients together with a wooden spoon, turn out the dough to a lightly-floured surface and knead about 5 times.
* Form the dough into a ball and place on a greased cookie sheet. Flatten out to about 1 inch.
* Cut into wedges, separate the wedges 1 inch, and bake 15 to 20 minutes or until golden brown.

Variations:

TYPE OF SCONE	MIX WITH THE #1 INGREDIENTS	MIX WITH THE #2 INGREDIENTS
Banana Scones	¾ cup sugar	Omit the buttermilk and add 1 cup banana, mashed, and 1 cup sour cream
Blueberry Scones	¾ cup sugar	1 cup fresh blueberries, or 1 cup frozen, defrosted and drained
Cheese and Onion Scones	You can also use cooked meats. Add 1 cup meat, diced	½ cup green onions, thinly sliced and 2 cups sharp cheddar cheese, shredded
Cream Scones	½ cup sugar	Omit the buttermilk and add 1 cup heavy cream
Orange Scones		Omit the buttermilk, and add 1 cup orange marmalade, 3 tablespoons milk if needed, and 1 cup golden raisins
Rich Chocolate Scones	¾ cup cocoa powder, and 1 cup brown sugar, loosely packed	¾ cup semi-sweet chocolate chips
Spicy Hot Seedy Scones	¼ teaspoon each: black pepper, cayenne pepper, and 1 tablespoon sugar. And, add 1 tablespoon each: poppy seeds and sesame seeds	
Tea Scones	¼ cup sugar, 1 tablespoon orange or lemon zest, and ¼ teaspoon cinnamon (optional)	1 cup raisins or currants

Chapter 20

MUFFINS

There are several important things to remember. Don't overmix. You can end up with cracks, peeks, and valleys. Overmixing develops the gluten in the flour, which is fine for yeast breads, but you can end up with a tough muffin. Mix with as few strokes as possible. Think in terms of folding the ingredients together rather than stirring or beating. The following will give you an idea of the temperature and times for different sized muffins.

SIZE	TEMPERATURE	YIELD
Regular $1\frac{3}{4}$ x 1-inch	400°	About 12
Large $3\frac{1}{2}$ x $1\frac{1}{2}$-inch	375°	4
Small 1 x 2-inch	350°	About 24

Always use vegetable spray in the muffin tins before adding the batter. For regular-sized muffins, fill the cups $\frac{2}{3}$ full. If you don't have enough batter for all the cups, put water in the empty ones to prevent scorching. The muffins need to bake for 10 to 15 minutes or until an inserted toothpick comes out clean.

If making colossal muffins, spray the top of the muffin tins, not just the inside of the cups. Fill the cups almost to the top. Do the same for the mini muffins. Let the muffins cool 3 to 5 minutes before removing from the tins.

Streusel Topping

#1 Ingredients
$\frac{1}{4}$ cup all-purpose flour
2 tablespoons packed brown sugar

2 tablespoons firm butter or
   margarine
$\frac{1}{4}$ teaspoon cinnamon
1 tablespoon nuts, chopped small

• Mix the #1 ingredients until crumbly. Sprinkle each muffin with 2 teaspoons topping and bake. This can be used on any sweet muffin.

Basic Muffins

FOR SWEET MUFFINS AND OTHER INGREDIENTS SEE **VARIATIONS** BELOW.

Preheat oven to 400°

#1 Ingredients
1 cup all-purpose flour
1 cup whole wheat flour or any
    bran or specialty flour
3 teaspoons baking powder
1/2 teaspoon salt

#2 Ingredients
1 cup milk
2 tablespoons oil (optional)
1 egg, beaten

- Mix the #1 ingredients with a fork. Mix the #2 ingredients with a fork.
- Pour into prepared muffin tins and bake for 10 to 15 minutes or until an inserted toothpick comes out clean.

You'll find in this recipe that I have 2 tablespoons of oil (optional).I never use oil because I don't want the added fat, and have found my muffins to be just as moist. Give it a try and see what you think.

Variations:
Sweet and Savory Muffins

SWEET MUFFINS	MIX WITH THE #1 INGREDIENTS	MIX WITH THE #2 INGREDIENTS
Apple Cinnamon Muffins	1/2 cup sugar and 1 teaspoon cinnamon	1 cup Granny Smith apples, peeled and diced
Banana Nut Muffins	1/2 cup sugar	1 cup banana, mashed, 1 cup nuts, your choice, chopped
Blueberry Muffins	1/2 cup sugar	1 cup fresh or frozen blueberries
Coconut and Macadamia Nut Muffins	1/4 cup sugar	1 cup coconut, shredded, and 1 cup macadamia nuts, chopped small
Cranberry Nut and Orange Muffins	1/2 cup sugar and 1 tablespoon orange zest	1 cup cranberries and 1 cup nuts, chopped (your choice)
Date Nut Muffins	1/2 cup sugar	1 cup dates, chopped and 1 cup walnuts, chopped
Double Chocolate Muffins	2/3 cup sugar and 5 tablespoons cocoa powder	1 cup semi-sweet chocolate chips

SWEET MUFFINS	MIX WITH THE #1 INGREDIENTS	MIX WITH THE #2 INGREDIENTS
Honey Nut Muffins		½ cup honey and 1 cup pecans, chopped
Lemon Poppy Seed Muffins	⅔ cup sugar, 3 tablespoons lemon zest and 3 tablespoons poppy seeds	½ teaspoon lemon extract
Mango Nut Muffins	½ cup sugar	1 cup fresh mango, diced, and add any juice you might collect while cutting up the mango plus ½ cup pecans, chopped
Maple Nut Muffins		Use ¾ cup milk, ½ cup maple syrup, ½ teaspoon maple extract, and 1 cup nuts, your choice, chopped
Orange Marmalade Muffins		1½ cups orange marmalade
Peanut Butter Muffins	½ cup sugar	½ cup peanut butter and 1 cup peanuts, chopped
Pear Muffins	½ cup sugar	1 cup fresh pears, peeled and diced and 1 tablespoon lemon zest
Pineapple Coconut Muffins	¼ cup sugar	⅔ cups fresh or frozen pineapple, diced and drained, and ½ cup coconut, shredded
Raspberry Muffins	½ cup sugar	1 cup fresh or frozen raspberries

SAVORY MUFFINS	MIX WITH THE #1 INGREDIENTS	MIX WITH THE #2 INGREDIENTS
Bacon Cheese and Onion Muffins		6 slices bacon, diced, fried, and drained, 1 cup shredded mozzarella cheese and 1/4 cup onion, diced small
Celery Cheese Muffins		1 cup provolone cheese, shredded, and 1 cup celery, sliced, sautéed, and drained
Cheese and Zucchini Muffins		1 cup raw zucchini, grated and drained on a paper towel, and 1 cup longhorn cheese, shredded
Cheesy Herbed Corn Muffins	Replace 1 cup all-purpose flour with 1 cup yellow cornmeal and 1/2 tablespoon each: dried basil and oregano	1 cup sharp cheddar cheese, shredded
Cheesy Sesame Chicken Muffins		1 cup cooked chicken, diced small, 1 cup longhorn cheese, shredded, and 1 teaspoon toasted sesame oil
Mushrooms, Cheese and Chives Muffins		Sauté and drain 1 cup mushrooms, diced small, add 1/2 cup chives, sliced thin, and 1 cup American cheese, shredded
Pizza Muffin		1 cup pepperoni, diced, fried, and drained, and 2 cups mozzarella cheese, shredded
Sausage and Cheese Muffins		1 cup mild sausage, cooked and drained, and 2 cups American cheese, shredded
Spinach Onion and Cheese Muffins		1 cup mild cheddar cheese, shredded, 1/2 cup onion, diced, and 1 cup fresh spinach, packed and chopped
Tuna and Cheese Muffins		1 6-ounce can tuna, packed in water and drained, and 2 cups Colby cheese, shredded

These are just a few ideas on what you can put in a muffin. Using these basic guidelines try some of your own ideas and have some fun.

Chapter 21

POPOVERS

For whopper popover soup bowls, double the recipe and use colossal size muffin tins. Grease and fill each cup half full. Bake at 450° for 30 minutes, and at 350° for 20 minutes. Then turn the oven off and let the popovers sit in the oven for at least 10 minutes. This will dry them out. Slice the top off with a sharp bread knife and serve your soup right in the popover. It's better to choose a thick soup.

Easy Popovers

TO USE OTHER INGREDIENTS SEE **VARIATIONS** BELOW.

Preheat oven to 450°

MAKES 6 POPOVERS

#1 Ingredients
1 cup all purpose flour
2 eggs, beaten
1 tablespoon olive oil
1 cup milk

#2 Ingredient
to be used with **Variations**

• Using your electric mixer on high, beat the #1 ingredients until smooth (the batter will be very thin). If using **Variations**, mix the #1 and #2 ingredients together using a wooden spoon.
• Pour into greased muffin tins so that each cup is 1/2 full.
• Bake at 450° for 20 minutes and turn oven to 350° and bake another 20 minutes. Turn off the oven and let the popovers sit in the oven another 5 minutes.

Important Note: Don't open the oven door during baking time or the popovers can fall.

Variations:

TYPE OF POPOVER	MIX WITH THE #1 INGREDIENTS	MIX WITH THE #2 INGREDIENTS
Cheese Popover		1 cup mild cheddar cheese, shredded
Cheesy Italian Popover	1 teaspoon Italian seasoning	1 cup mozzarella cheese, shredded
Chives and Cheese Popover		1/2 cup fresh chives, sliced thin or 1/4 cup, dried and 1 cup Colby cheese, shredded
Garlic Popover	1 tablespoon garlic, minced	
Ham and Cheese Popover		1/2 cup smoked ham, diced very small and 1/4 cup Parmesan cheese, grated
Mustard, Cheese, and Onion Popover	1 tablespoon prepared mustard, your choice	1/2 cup green onions, sliced thin, and 1/2 cup Swiss cheese, shredded
Pecan Popover		1/2 cup pecans, minced
Pepper Popover	1 tablespoon black pepper, freshly ground	
Whole Wheat Popover	Replace the all-purpose flour with whole wheat flour	

Chapter 22

BREAD STICKS AND CRACKERS

Basic Bread Sticks

TO USE OTHER INGREDIENTS SEE **VARIATIONS** ON PAGE 199.

Preheat oven to 400°

MAKES 12 TO 16 BREAD STICKS

#1 Ingredients
3 cups all-purpose flour
3 teaspoons baking powder
1 teaspoon salt

#2 Ingredients
2 tablespoons melted butter or
    margarine
1 cup milk
1 egg, beaten

- Mix the #1 ingredients together with a wire whisk. Mix the #2 ingredients with a wire whisk.
- Mix the #1 and #2 ingredients until you have smooth stiff dough, adding more flour or water if need be.
- Flour your hands and knead 10 times on a floured surface. Flour your rolling pin and roll dough out to ½ inch thick. Cut into strips ½ inch wide.
- Put on a cookie sheet that has been sprayed with cooking spray, keeping the strips at least ½ inch apart. Bake 10 to 15 minutes or until golden brown.

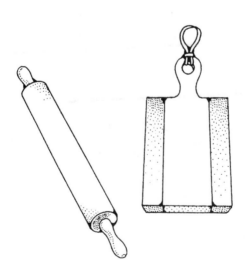

Variations:

TYPE OF BREAD STICKS	MIX WITH THE #1 INGREDIENTS	MIX WITH THE #2 INGREDIENTS
Cheesy Onion Bread Sticks		1/2 cup green onion, sliced thin, and 2 cups sharp cheddar cheese, shredded
Italian Sesame Seed Bread Sticks	4 teaspoons Italian seasoning, 3 tablespoons toasted sesame seeds, and 1/2 teaspoon garlic powder	(Egg wash) Beat 1 egg, with 1 tablespoon water, brush each stick with the egg wash and sprinkle with sesame seeds and brush with egg wash again. This egg wash may be used on any bread stick with your choice of topping.
Poppy and Parmesan Cheese Bread Sticks	3 tablespoons poppy seeds and 1/2 cup Parmesan cheese, grated	
Rye, Caraway and Cheese Bread Sticks	Replace 1 1/2 cups all purpose flour with 1 1/2 cups rye flour and 2 tablespoons caraway seeds	2 cups mozzarella cheese, shredded
Tomato, Basil and Garlic Bread Sticks		2 teaspoons garlic, minced, 1 teaspoon tomato paste, 3 tablespoons fresh basil, minced

Crackers

Preheat oven to 425°

MAKES 2 DOZEN CRACKERS

#1 Ingredients
2 cups all-purpose flour
1 teaspoon salt

#2 Ingredients
2/3 cup milk

- Mix the #1 ingredients together with a wire whisk. Mix the #1 and #2 ingredients, using a wooden spoon, until you have a smooth stiff dough. Knead on a floured surface 10 to 15 times and roll out as thin as possible.
- Cut into squares and poke each square several times with a fork. Place on a cookie sheet that has been sprayed with cooking spray and bake for 6 to 8 minutes.

Variations:

TYPE OF CRACKER	MIX WITH THE #1 INGREDIENTS	MIX WITH THE #2 INGREDIENTS
Barbecue Crackers		2 tablespoons barbecue sauce (your choice)
Blue Corn Crackers	Replace 1 cup all-purpose flour with 1 cup blue cornmeal or regular cornmeal, 1 tablespoon chili powder	
Bran Crackers	Replace 1/2 cup all purpose flour with 1/2 cup raw oat bran	
Celery Seed Crackers	2 tablespoons celery seeds	
Chili Crackers	3 tablespoons chili mix (from the envelope)	
Cinnamon Sugar Crackers		Use basic recipe and after crackers are baked brush lightly with melted butter and sprinkle with cinnamon sugar, stick under the broiler for just seconds, until the sugar starts to brown
Cumin Crackers	2 tablespoons cumin seeds	
Curry Crackers	1 tablespoon curry powder	

TYPE OF CRACKER	MIX WITH THE #1 INGREDIENTS	MIX WITH THE #2 INGREDIENTS
Dill Crackers	2 tablespoons dried dill weed	
Garlic Crackers		1/2 tablespoon garlic, minced
Italian Crackers	1 tablespoon Italian seasoning	
Lemon Pepper Crackers	3 tablespoons lemon pepper	
Mustard and Chive Crackers	3 tablespoons dried chives	2 tablespoons sweet and hot mustard or your choice
Onion Crackers	2 tablespoons dried onion flakes	
Parmesan Cheese Crackers	1/4 cup Parmesan cheese, grated	
Rye and Caraway Seed Crackers	Replace 1 cup all-purpose flour with 1 cup rye flour, and 1/2 tablespoon caraway seeds	
Sesame or Poppyseed Crackers (try using both in the same crackers)	4 tablespoons seeds	When using sesame seeds add 1 teaspoon toasted sesame oil
Taco Crackers	3 tablespoons taco seasoning (from the envelope)	
Whole Wheat and Wheat Germ Crackers	Replace 1 cup all-purpose flour with 1 cup whole wheat flour, and 4 tablespoons wheat germ	

Chapter 23

FRITTERS

Corn Fritters

MAKES 12 TO 16 FRITTERS

#1 Ingredients
1 cup all-purpose flour
½ teaspoon salt
½ tablespoon sugar

#2 Ingredients
1 cup frozen corn, defrosted
2 eggs, beaten
3 tablespoons fresh lemon juice
⅔ cup milk

#3 Ingredient
oil 2 inches deep in your frying pan

- Mix the #1 ingredients together with a wire whisk. Mix the #2 ingredients together with a fork.
- Mix the #1 and #2 ingredients together. Let batter rest while the oil heats up.
- Dip your tablespoon in the hot oil to lubricate your spoon and drop the batter a tablespoon at a time into the hot oil. The fritters will float to the top when almost done. Turn over to complete browning. Drain on a paper towel and serve warm.

Goes well with 1 cup salsa mixed with 1 cup sour cream for dipping.

Ham Fritters

MAKES 12 TO 16 FRITTERS

#1 Ingredients
1 cup all-purpose flour
½ teaspoon salt

#3 Ingredient
oil 2 inches deep in your frying pan

#2 Ingredients
½ cup smoked ham, diced very small
2 eggs, beaten
⅔ cup milk

- Mix the #1 ingredients together with a wire whisk. Mix the #2 ingredients together with a fork until very well blended.
- Mix the #1 and #2 ingredients together. Let batter rest while the oil heats up.
- Dip your spoon in the hot oil to lubricate it and drop the batter a tablespoon at a time into the hot oil. The fritters will float to the top when almost done. Turn over to complete browning. Drain on a paper towel and serve warm.

Beer and Onion Fritters

THIS ONE HAS TO REST FOR AT LEAST TWO HOURS COVERED
IN THE FRIDGE, BUT IS WORTH IT IF YOU HAVE THE TIME.

MAKES 12 TO 16 FRITTERS

#1 Ingredients
2 cups all-purpose flour
1 teaspoon salt

#2 Ingredients
1 cup beer
2 eggs, beaten
3/4 cup milk
1 tablespoon melted butter

#3 Ingredient
1/2 cup onion, diced very small

#4 Ingredient
oil 2 inches deep in your frying pan

- Mix the #1 ingredients together with a wire whisk. Mix the #2 ingredients together with a wire whisk.
- Mix the #1 and #2 ingredients together.
- Let batter rest for two hours covered in the fridge. This allows the batter to ferment and gives it a better consistency.
- Remix the batter and add the #3 ingredients. Dip your tablespoon in the hot oil to lubricate it and drop the batter a tablespoon at a time into the hot oil. The fritters will float to the top when almost done. Turn over to complete browning. Drain on a paper towel and serve warm.

Hush Puppies

MAKES 12 TO 16 FRITTERS

#1 Ingredients
1 1/2 cups white or yellow corn
meal
1/2 cup all-purpose flour
1 teaspoon baking powder
1/2 teaspoon baking soda
1/2 teaspoon salt
1/2 teaspoon onion powder

#2 Ingredients
2/3 cup buttermilk
1 egg, beaten
1/4 cup onion, grated

#3 Ingredient
oil 2 inches deep in your frying
pan

- Mix the #1 ingredients together with a wire whisk. Mix the #2 ingredients together with a wire whisk.
- Mix the #1 and #2 ingredients together with a wooden spoon. Let the batter rest while the oil heats up.
- Dip your spoon in the hot oil to lubricate it. Drop the batter into the hot oil one tablespoon at a time. The fritters will float to the top when almost done. Turn over to complete the browning. Drain on a paper towel and serve warm.

Apple Fritters

MAKES 12 TO 16 FRITTERS

#1 Ingredients
1 cup all-purpose flour
½ teaspoon salt
1 tablespoon sugar
½ teaspoon cinnamon

#2 Ingredients
1 cup Granny Smith apples,
    peeled and diced very small
2 eggs, beaten
⅔ cup milk
1 tablespoon melted butter

#3 Ingredient
oil 2 inches deep in your frying
pan

- Mix the #1 ingredients together with a wire whisk. Mix the #2 ingredients together with a fork.
- Mix the #1 and #2 ingredients together. Let batter rest while the oil heats up.
- Dip your spoon in the hot oil to lubricate it and drop the batter a tablespoon at a time into the hot oil. The fritters will float to the top when almost done. Turn over to complete browning. Drain on a paper towel and serve warm.

Banana Fritters

MAKES 12 TO 16 FRITTERS

#1 Ingredients
1 cup all-purpose flour
½ teaspoon salt
1 tablespoon sugar

#2 Ingredients
½ cup bananas, diced small (not
    over-ripe, they have to hold
    their shape)
2 eggs, beaten
⅔ cup milk

#3 Ingredient
oil 2 inches deep in your frying pan

- Mix the #1 ingredients together with a wire whisk. Mix the #2 ingredients together with a fork.
- Mix the #1 and #2 ingredients together. Let batter rest while the oil heats up.
- Dip your tablespoon in the hot oil to lubricate your spoon and drop the batter a tablespoon at a time into the hot oil. The fritters will float to the top when almost done. Turn over to complete browning. Drain on a paper towel and serve warm.

Sweet Little Honey Puffs

MAKES 12 TO 16 FRITTERS

#1 Ingredients
2 cups all-purpose flour
3 teaspoons baking powder
1 teaspoon baking soda
1 teaspoon salt
¼ teaspoon nutmeg
¼ teaspoon cinnamon

#2 Ingredients
3 eggs, beaten
3 tablespoons melted butter
1 cup sour cream

#3 Ingredient
oil 2 inches deep in your frying
  pan

#4 Ingredient
1 cup honey (for dipping)

- Mix the #1 ingredients together with a wire whisk. Mix the #2 ingredients together with a wire whisk.
- Mix the #1 and #2 ingredients together. Let the batter rest while the oil heats up.
- Dip your tablespoon in the hot oil to lubricate it and drop the batter a tablespoon at a time into the hot oil. The fritters will float to the top when almost done. Turn over to complete browning. Drain on a paper towel, and serve warm.

Chapter 24

FLAT BREADS

Chapati Indian Flat Bread

MAKES 15 FLAT BREADS

#1 Ingredients
1¾ cups whole wheat flour
¾ cup all-purpose flour

#2 Ingredient
¾ cup water

- Mix #1 and #2 ingredients into a soft dough, place on a floured surface, adding flour or water as needed.
- Flour your hands and knead 15 times or until the dough is smooth. Add more flour as needed. Cover with a warm damp cloth and let rest for 30 minutes.
- Divide dough into 15 balls, dust hands and rolling pin with flour, and roll out to 5½ inches in diameter. Dust with flour as needed.
- Slap flattened bread between your floured hands several times, and place in a skillet that's been sprayed with cooking spray and heated to a medium heat. Cook on a low heat until lightly brown on one side. After 1 to 2 minutes turn and cook on the other side until brown. Serve.

Sri Lankan Flat Bread

MAKES 15 FLAT BREADS

#1 Ingredients
2½ cups all-purpose flour
1 cup coconut, finely shredded
2 teaspoons baking powder

#2 Ingredient
1¼ cups water

- Mix #1 and #2 ingredients into a soft dough and place on a floured surface. Flour your hands and knead 15 times or until the dough is smooth, adding more flour or water if needed.
- Cover with a warm damp cloth and let rest 30 minutes. Divide into 15 balls, dust hands and rolling pin with flour and roll out to 5½ inch in diameter, dusting with flour as needed.
- Slap flattened bread between your floured hands several times. Place in a skillet that's been sprayed with cooking spray and heated to a medium heat.
- Cook on a low heat until lightly brown on one side for about 1 to 2 minutes. Turn and cook on the other side until brown. Serve.

Native American Buckskin Bread

THIS IS A SIMPLE FLAT BREAD THAT'S FAST AND BAKED IN A PIE SHELL.

Preheat oven to 400°

MAKES 2 FLAT BREADS

Thanks to my buddy Tom, author of *The Medicine Man.*

#1 Ingredients
4 cups all-purpose flour
2¼ teaspoons baking powder
1½ teaspoons salt

#2 Ingredient
2 cups water

- Mix the #1 ingredients with a wire whisk. Mix the #1 and #2 ingredients together to form a dough. Divide in half, flatten into two greased 9-inch pie plates, and bake for 25 minutes or until golden brown.

Czechoslovakian Fry Bread (Milosti)

MAKES ABOUT 24 SQUARES

#1 Ingredients
3 cups all-purpose flour
½ cup sugar
⅛ teaspoon salt
⅛ teaspoon mace
zest from ½ lemon

#2 Ingredients
3 eggs, beaten
½ cup heavy cream

#3 Ingredient
oil 2 inches deep in your frying pan

#4 Ingredient
sugar for sprinkling

- Mix the #1 ingredients together with a wire whisk. Mix the #2 ingredients together with a wire whisk.
- Mix the #1 and the #2 ingredients together with a wooden spoon and knead 5 times on a floured surface. Roll out to ⅛ inch thick and cut into squares.
- Heat oil in a medium-sized skillet until almost smoking. Turn heat to medium. Fry both sides until golden brown, turning over once. Sprinkle with the #4 ingredient while still wet from the oil and serve.

Pepper Flat Bread

MAKES 15 FLAT BREADS

#1 Ingredients
¾ cup all-purpose flour
½ teaspoon crushed black pepper

#2 Ingredient
¾ cup water

- Mix the #1 and #2 ingredients into a soft dough and place on a floured surface. Flour your hands and knead 15 times or until the dough is smooth. Add more flour or water if needed. Cover with a warm damp cloth and let rest 30 minutes.
- Divide into 15 balls, dust hands and rolling pin with flour, and roll out to 5 ½ inches in diameter. Dust with flour as needed.
- Slap flattened bread between your floured hands several times. Place in a skillet that's been sprayed with cooking spray and heated to a medium heat. Turn to low heat and cook until lightly brown on one side, about 1 to 2 minutes. Then turn and cook on the other side until brown. Serve.

Tsung Yu Ping Flat Bread
Chinese Onion Circles

MAKES 15 FLAT BREADS

#1 Ingredients
3 cups all-purpose flour
2 teaspoons baking powder
1 teaspoon salt
1 cup green onions, sliced very thin

#2 Ingredients
1 cup water
1 tablespoon sesame seed oil

- Mix the #1 and #2 ingredients into a soft dough, and place on a floured surface. Flour your hands and knead 15 times or until the dough is smooth. Add more flour or water if necessary. Cover with a warm damp cloth and let rest 30 minutes.
- Divide into 15 balls, dust hands and rolling pin with flour and roll out to 5 ½ inches in diameter, dusting with flour as needed.
- Slap flattened bread between your floured hands several times. Place in a skillet that's been sprayed with cooking spray and heated to a medium heat. Cook on a low heat until lightly brown on one side for about 1 to 2 minutes. Turn and cook on the other side until brown. Serve.

INDEX

S